Case for the Conservative

Case for the Conservative

James S. Munn

Copyright © 2011 by Seneca Associates, Inc.

Library of Congress Control Number: 2011911739
ISBN: Hardcover   978-1-4628-9160-3
             Softcover   978-1-4628-9159-7
             Ebook   978-1-4628-9161-0

All rights reserved. No part of this book may be reproduced or transmitted in any form or by any means, electronic or mechanical, including photocopying, recording, or by any information storage and retrieval system, without permission in writing from the copyright owner.

This book was printed in the United States of America.

To order additional copies of this book, contact:
Xlibris Corporation
1-888-795-4274
www.Xlibris.com
Orders@Xlibris.com
98909

CONTENTS

Preface 7
Introduction 9

I	The Nature of Things 15
II	The Conservative Estate 28
III	Conservative Identification 32
IV	Anatomy of Liberty and Property 36
V	Opportunity, Education, and the Law 59
VI	Concept of Government 78
VII	Economic Growth, Abundance, and the Estate 83
VIII	Underemployment and the State 100
IX	Individual Mobility: Self-reliance and Dependence 123
X	Security and Conservation of the State 141
XI	The Special Problem of the Counterrevolution[72] 165
XII	The Part Assigned to Us 183
XIII	Where Do We Go From Here? 189

Endnotes 197
Index 211

PREFACE

This nation, under God, shall have a new birth of freedom . . .

—Abraham Lincoln

Endowed by their creator with certain inalienable rights . . .

—Declaration of Independence

The independence of individual Americans is declared on the foundation of equality under law and basic human rights. Rights are inalienable precisely because they are endowed by their creator.

So long as we retain the wisdom, the courage, and the strength to preserve "the sovereign authority of this nation as the sanctuary of liberty," so long as we have the fortitude to sustain this temple to our faith wherever, and so long as men embrace liberty, they will turn their faces and hearts toward us. The more they multiply, the more friends we will have; the more ardently they love liberty, the more perfect will be their dedication.

"Slavery may be had anywhere. It is the weed that grows in any soil." But until we become lost to all feeling of our *true interest* and our *national dignity*, freedom they can have from none—except us.

On the day that we forsake the idea that man is the creature of God, on that day, all our resources, affluence, and power will be but as a fragile reed before the totalitarian tempest sweeping the world.

Only under God is man free. Only under God can a nation project this freedom in liberty through a legal system and institutions to protect and not abridge man's inalienable rights.

It is the Conservative who stands in solitary defense of these noble traditions and forms. The embattled defenses stand assailed by radical reform and reaction alike.

This is a restatement of the American Conservative position. Like Jefferson, I do not consider it my role to "invent new ideas" and to present a "sentiment" that has never been expressed before. It is my intention here to place before the reader "the common sense of it."

Introduction

This attempt at a restatement of the American Conservative position is influenced by the fact that I am an adherent to that position. Unable to obtain a position of exclusive detachment from my understandings and beliefs, I acknowledge them and proceed. In reflection, I have discovered these beliefs to be influenced by several unshakable recollections.

During World War II, I was a B-17 pilot flying bombing missions over Europe. I was shot down, captured in Nazi Germany, and remained a Prisoner of War for approximately one and a half years. During this period, I had a limited opportunity to witness the operations of the Nazi regime.

The curtain came down on this spectacle when we broke out of the prison camp in the closing days of the war. We used our liberty to free some less fortunate concentration camp inmates in the area. The stench was overpowering. The sight of these dehumanized beings left an impression on me that lingers to this day.

Shortly after we broke out of our camp, I had my first view of the Red Army. These were Mongolian troops under European Russian officers. Even as one discounts the rights of battle and the flush of victory, these were barbaric troops by our standards. They were literally living off of the land, raping, pillaging, and terrorizing as they moved across the north German countryside. To discount this as the natural product of war, one would have to ignore the stringent discipline of the officers and the presence of the political commissar.

Immediately following the occupation of the territory, the process of liquidation of "undesirable" members of the civilian population began. I shall never forget the picture on a lonely beach of five adult corpses, two minor children, and an infant in a baby carriage, all in a row, face to the sky, killed by the gun of a Communist executioner.

Not long afterward, I returned to my native state of California and went to Camp Beal in the Sacramento Valley prior to going home for a rest. While there, I had occasion to go into a small grocery store for a purchase. Over the counter, there was a sign No Dogs or Japanese Allowed. I was outraged and a little sickened. I remarked on this and was reminded that this was only to be expected. Had I forgotten that thousands of our Japanese neighbors had been evicted from their homes and placed in detention camps? I did recall, but my awareness was that from four years before, as a youth of nineteen going off to war. The impression was faint, and only now did I appreciate the enormity.

Although I talked often about my wartime impressions and my apprehensions for the future, the sharpness of my perception was blunted; the clarity of my vision was clouded by peace. Peace—it was wonderful. The years that followed were personal years. I spent my time trying to recover the years I had missed. This was the occupational disease of the returning veteran. The revelation that some of the old college fraternities excluded Jewish persons from their membership disturbed me little.

The Korean War came, and I was recalled to service. Months later, on a day in May, I happened to be in Tokyo. There, I was exposed for the first time to the sight of an apparently uncontrolled mob running through the streets, beating, burning, and terrorizing. These were the Socialists and the Communists, and they were celebrating May Day. My memory was propelled back to a time in my youth when the San Francisco waterfront was terrorized by striking workmen. I remembered the barbed wire barricades, the soldiers, and the marauding bands of strikers who had taken the law into their own hands. The impression was strong.

I returned to the United States and was assigned to an air force base in Central Louisiana. My arrival corresponded with the heightening crisis associated with the Supreme Court desegregation decision. "White Citizens' Councils" were becoming active. These were militant groups intended to give expression to a desire to retain racial segregation. So long as the organization retained its essential law-abiding character, I was undisturbed.

One night, returning from a hunting trip with some friends, I was exposed to a sight I will not forget. In the basement of one of these friends' home was an arsenal, not an arsenal of sporting weapons but an arsenal of military weapons. No secret was made of the fact that these arms were cached in the event that resistance to desegregation legally should fail. I was startled but, I must confess, not too much surprised.

About this time, a young black boy from a northern city was visiting his aunt in nearby Mississippi. He was arrested after having allegedly made some obscene remarks to a white woman. One night, he was forcibly taken from his jail cell by a mob and did not return alive. The community seemed little disturbed by the action of the mob. To my knowledge, no one was ever held accountable. For the first time in my life, I began to feel insecure within the land that I regarded as the haven of liberty.

Military service ended. I left the struggling South behind. I moved to the Pacific Northwest, where I lived in comfort and relative tranquility with my family for several years.

One episode of this period remains strong in my memory. This was during a time when the "right to work" laws were generating much concern on the part of labor union management. One day, I was engaged in conversation with an official of one of our most powerful and proudly democratic industrial unions. This man had returned from a national convention where substantial opposition to the national leadership had developed. With an element of pride, this man related how efficiently the dissenters had been physically ejected from the convention hall. He was positive in his indictment of the opposition as self-seeking persons who should be tried before the "executive board" for "un-union-like conduct."

In recent years, these instances and others within my experience have had a substantial influence on the formation of my thinking. There was one aspect of the circumstances surrounding each incident common to all. This was the ready disposition to employ force in the place of law to achieve the objective, which the parties involved justified by their particular bias. This was true of the Nazi, the Communist, the Socialist, the Segregationist, the Trade Unionist, and the Liberal.

One question demanded an answer: were they all the same? The answer was not difficult to determine. Abundant evidence indicated fundamental distinctions that no conspicuous similarities could obscure.

Was it true that the Fascist is distinct from the Communist; the Communist, from the Socialist; the Socialist, from the Liberal; etc.? Why then did each have a disturbingly similar disposition to take the law into its own hands? The answer to this question promised a possible solution to a dilemma that had bothered me for years. How can one pursue liberty and at the same time remain responsive to the compelling material needs of humanity?

While studying in Europe, I discovered an answer. This is not to imply that the answer was found to be outside America. Rather, it was the distance from the immediacy of American surroundings that allowed me the opportunity to reflect, to view the whole pattern, and to see my land in perspective.

I was profoundly influenced by the convulsions of France, bravely struggling to liquidate the "Algerian problem." The sight of midnight arrests of thousands of people in Paris, the cradle of "Liberté, égalité, fraternité," forced one to recall the terror of the revolution and all subsequent convulsions. Who could remain untouched by such tragedies flowing from such noble traditions?

I viewed the chaos in the Congo, where the United Nations was busy seeking to reduce the province of Katanga to the control of a "central government," itself unable to control even the savage behavior of its own armed forces. The glowing principles of "self-determination" seemed lost in the preoccupation of the planners, with the economic consequences of continued provincial autonomy.

One day, contemplating the apparently remarkable recovery of West Germany from the tragedy of National Socialism and total defeat in World War II, I was struck by a central realization. The answer was clear. It cried out to be recognized. The facts were all present and fitted without exception. Despite all distinctions of method, of plan, of program, and of trappings, the common characteristics of all were a dogmatic concept of man's ultimate or ideal condition and an acceptance that the achievement of the end was all the justification required to support the means to be employed. All shared the common position that the end justifies the means[1].

Armed with this realization, I pondered the significance as I sought to relate this central fact to the main political questions that command our attention. Considering each developed political position, I found that all, except the Conservative, had a plan. All who advanced these plans manifested the ethical, or perhaps more accurately, nonethical belief that the end justified the means must each be measured against established, consistent, traditional ethical standards. It was the Conservative position that was under assault from every side.

When this fact became clear, everything began to take on form and meaning; the enigma began to disappear. I had learned the central political truth. There are only Conservatives and non-Conservatives.

The non-Conservatives are a fractioned lot. They operate under the banners of Communism, Fascism, Socialism, Fabianism, Liberalism, Nazism, Provincialism, Metropolitanism, Nationalism, Internationalism, Individualism, or any kind of "-ism" with a plan, a dogma, and a readiness to achieve the goal of the plan over all opposition, employing any means available, efficient, and effective.

This, then, is the problem. Starting from the central premise—there are only Conservatives and non-Conservatives—identification and differentiation is the task.

THE NATURE OF THINGS

It behooves us to take care that our opinions are according to the nature of things.

—Benjamin Franklin

It is our habit to rely heavily upon stereotypes to facilitate our thinking. It is at least difficult to employ more discriminating techniques of consideration. Could we have but realized that stereotypes are useful but are not real and could we have always remembered that they are but abstractions with limited utility, we would have progressed far. The important thing to remember is that each abstraction has a very special purpose, and when carelessly employed outside the proper frame of reference, there is immediately raised the risk of serious error.

This matter of the use of stereotypes and abstractions becomes of great importance in framing our political judgments. Recognition of the use of the stereotype by the "popular" leader is the first step in the essential discount process. The particular terminology employed or the technical definitions of the words are not nearly as significant as knowing what he and we are talking about.

The human being seems to have a built-in capacity for emotional response to abstract terminology. The terms themselves tend to develop an emotional charge that induces an automatic response in the listener whenever he is exposed to them. When these terms are employed by the politician in popular appeal in the course of a general political debate, they become a substitute for substance, and sound political judgment is thereby inhibited. The general political "debate" of the presidential election of 1960 was a clear example of the phenomenon. The abstractions of *missile gap*, *growth rate*, *population explosion*, *depressed area*, *underprivileged*, *national prestige*, *New Frontier*, and *move ahead* were all freely employed for the purpose of influencing political judgments on the basis of emotional bias, not fact and reason. These ill-defined, imprecise, obscure, abstract phrases were all employed outside the appropriate frame of reference with telling effect. They had particular utility to the non-Conservative Liberal politician in facilitating the bid for power.

The phrases are all high-sounding, indeed. Consider the voter who had never looked at an economics textbook: all at once he found himself an expert on economics. All could see that the economic uncertainties to which the individual was exposed were explained by the simple "fact" that the *growth rate* had not been sufficient during the preceding administration. The choice was thus simplified. Elect the candidate who had identified the deficiency and expressed a determination to "move the nation ahead" to overcome the "growth rate" deficit.

The fact that so many American voters are seduced by just such diversions and distortions does not make the perpetrator of the fraud any less culpable. A casual dismissal of the fraud as but another evidence of a characteristic of the "democratic" process or a sophisticated rationalization that "after all, no intelligent person really believes campaign promises or oratory," just does not get to the root of the matter. The root of the matter is that if voters are induced to exercise their franchise for or against a particular candidate on the basis of guile, deception, invention, pretense, and sham, their "democratic" right has been embezzled from them.

The larceny is complete when the vote is cast, induced by the deceit. True enough, the politician may find that the bid for power is actually facilitated by the suppressions of fact, diversion from reality, and misrepresentation of issues. This is particularly true if the politician is not the incumbent or identified with the incumbent administration and has but one concept of responsibility, and that is to the bid for power. However, it is following the election that real public understanding is required. Here, there is no substitute for fact, and fact understood. The problem of separating fact from fancy is one of the most delicate problems that the elected official must face. It is absolutely the most difficult for the propagandized citizen.

Little would it profit us to judge here the degree that a particular politician had been seduced by the immense temptations of power to compromise with truth and veracity. Let history and another tribunal judge the merits of any quarrel between the leader and the led. Let us here address ourselves to the task to discover and understand the nature of things. Let us undertake the task in order that we may apply our judgments and energies toward the constructive development of our society.

There may have been a period of American history when it was reasonably harmless to entertain the delusion of the "pie in the sky," that it was not really necessary to "pay the piper" to dance to the tune. Today, when the specter of extinction stalks us as a shadow, this is a comfortable luxury that none can afford. If we are to have a meaningful influence on mankind's future development, we must do away with the dreams of fancy and concentrate our critical attention on the facts of our existence, our current stage of development, and our prospects. It is only here that the answers will be found, which can serve as reliable guides down the tortuous path.

It would ill serve us indeed to gain the impression that labels are not useful at all. When we are in the process of ordering our thinking about a particular thing, their utility is great. To state on a summer's day that "it is hot" conveys a useful meaning. To be sure, this is not sufficiently precise to be of much use to the meteorologist, but it does give a general impression of the state of the temperature and our reaction to it. To say that "a man is a Republican" is somewhat the same as saying "it is hot." We get a general idea of his political "temperature," but we are left without much in the way of precise knowledge as to how he will act and react to certain situations calling for his political judgments. In fact, when we begin applying the labels of Democrat and Republican, we might easily ask ourselves if there is any use at all. We observe that each of the parties embrace political dispositions all over the spectrum. The only meaningful distinction appears to be between the "ins" and the "outs."

It is apparent that the broad representation within each of the major political parties precludes all but the most questionable judgments as to the nature of the ideas of government, which will find expression where the representative is elected on the basis of party label alone. How then is the citizen to judge if the commonly accepted label is potentially so misleading? The significant distinction today in these United States is between the Conservative and the non-Conservative.

How is this so? we might ask, when a "national leader" describes himself as a "Conservative with a heart" or that he is an "economic Conservative" but a "human Liberal." What in fact is meant by the term *Progressive Conservative*, and doesn't all meaning disappear when we are confronted by the term "*Liberal Conservative?*

Despite all of this apparent confusion, the distinctions are real and, once understood and consistently applied, will serve as a reliable guide to political action.

There is a fundamental distinction between the American Conservative and non-Conservative that no external resemblance will eclipse. The difference has its roots deep in antiquity and has persisted without substantial variation since the Conservative position was first confronted with its non-Conservative opposition. The distinction has to do with the basic concept of the nature of man. The non-Conservative generally believes the nature of man to be in some way perfectible. Quite simply, the Conservative believes that it is not susceptible to such change as to yield a calculated state of perfection.

Involved here is a basic divergence in the understanding of substance of freedom. To the non-Conservative, freedom consists of delivering oneself of individual wants, preferences, interests, ambitions, needs, and developing the all-embracing harmony and unanimity of the "general will"[2]. The objective of the non-Conservative political life is to mold the nature of man to a state where he will conform to the "general will" without need of coercion. Non-Conservative freedom becomes identified with a loss of the individual in the collective entity of the state where he accepts the interest and existence of the state as his own.

In the Conservative sense, freedom involves a fundamental identification and acceptance of God. The essence of the idea is that man cannot be free until he reaches an understanding of this relationship to the creative and final authority. Only when man stands in direct relationship to God does he become free from finite limitations. As long as man rejects the idea of a creative and final authority, he remains totally dependent upon his material environment, is forever subject to the absolute subordinating direction of the secular religion, and controls authority.

When man stands in direct relationship to the ultimate and eternal authority, he requires no intermediary between himself and his creator and judge. No institutional apparatus is required for man to realize the condition of direct relationship. All churches and ecclesiastics function only to facilitate the communion but are not basic to the fact of the communion itself.

It is in this context that the American Conservative understands the nature of freedom within the traditions of Western civilization. This is the concept that is fundamental to the Anglo-American legal systems and that has developed into the political institutions and forms of the United States.

This is the meaning of freedom as a natural condition of man that requires the maximum liberty to facilitate the fullest development of each according to his unique capabilities.

Some of the confusion that surrounds the basic Conservative position seems related to a failure to differentiate the nature of freedom from the concept of liberty. These are not just two terms describing the same thing. This is not a case of simple semantic preference.

The Conservative understands this but sometimes fails to distinguish in general usage. When the distinction becomes blurred, the force becomes blunted in social impact.

Freedom remains the natural, the essential condition of man. It is the condition of each human being as he stands in direct relationship to God. To the Christian, this begins with man-made freedom through reconciliation in Christ. God made man whole and therefore free.

Freedom involves man's conceptual capacity, his faculty of choice, and his delayed response to stimuli. In a profound sense, this radical freedom accounts for man's essential individuality and thus his apparent willfulness, his essential individuality, and his consequent unpredictability.

Liberty is corporal in nature. It is the state of the absence of coercive restraint. This involves all of the social and political liberties that are characteristic of the democratic republic. The concept is relative and a condition of social-political significance. The essence is a prevailing recognition of the necessity to provide a social environment and political organization that corresponds most nearly to the reality of freedom in man's nature.

Within this general framework, the fundamental distinctions between the Conservative and the non-Conservative are cogently considered. These distinctions relate to the basic concept of the nature of man (human nature). The non-Conservative believes this nature to be perfectible through environmental condition. Given the required environmental system, human nature is capable of development generation following upon generation. The Conservative knows this to be the myth upon which the whole totalitarian-democratic tradition is founded. The Conservative accepts the fact that man is endowed with his nature and that it does not lie within his capacity to change this nature in any manner except to rob it of the inherent human element.

The non-Conservative takes the "rational" approach to sociopolitical problems. Implicit is an unlimited confidence in the capacity of reason to solve all things. Underlying this confidence is a belief that through the application of intelligence, the root causes of all human willfulness can be identified, and once identified, rational and scientific planning and control over the social environment can eliminate the causes and thus the willfulness. The Conservative cannot accord such an exalted position to reason and intelligence.[3]

Man is an independent being capable of responses to stimuli through the exercise of the faculty of choice. Human nature is subject to frailties, is always fallible, and remains free to act in accord or contrary to man's real interests. It is the frailty and fallibility that is reflected in the apparent individual willfulness.

Each individual has the capacity to discipline his nature and thereby develop his personality and character so as to deal with tempting stimuli encountered through the period called life.

The Conservative understands it to be each individual's role to develop his personality and character to such a level that he lives a virtuous life, but the perfectibility of his nature lies beyond human capacity. The frailty and fallibility cannot be eliminated. There will be no "supermen" of the "ideal state." It remains the lot of each individual to struggle with his nature to achieve the maximum development lying within his unique capacities. Each person retains the responsibility for his own development and, in the final analysis, is judged by the final authority.

The Conservative idea has to do with development toward a virtuous state of being, which in no way involves a perfection of his nature. Each will be measured according to his merit, and this will not be measured by the "improvements" that he has "rationally" effected in the nature with which he is endowed. When this is placed alongside the non-Conservative concept that man's nature is of such malleable stuff that it can be molded from generation to generation to ultimately acquire characteristics comprehended in a planned state of perfection; such is of a base order when compared to the sublime idea of the Conservative.

The basic Conservative objection lies in the non-Conservative view that man is a malleable creature that can be molded by the laws and the institutions erected to proscribe and circumscribe his conduct. The American Conservative cannot accept that man is a product of his education in the broad sense, effecting reconciliation with a deduced universal moral order and truth. Man is much more than the product of the laws of the state, and any attempt by the state to form man into a predetermined pattern will lead to frustration and containment of potentially explosive forces.

This thesis is not dependent upon a belief that man exists under a burden of sin that has so corrupted his nature that he is all but incapable of salvation. The ideas of predestination have never had logical or emotional appeal to the American Conservative. God's grace is an inscrutable thing that cannot be so comprehended with such certainty that one needs but to conform to a system of behavior to earn a place. It is at least doubtful that one can bargain, as it were, with the omniscient, omnipotent authority.

Generally, the Conservative believes in God's grace and accepts that the dispensation is through his bounty and not the result of some crude equation between bad and good works. Man lives out his life responsibly and morally, not to earn salvation but for the love of God. There does not seem to be any conflict between this concept and the idea of innate goodness if what is meant is a nature capable of serving God through a virtuous life. There is a real conflict, however, with the idea of "innate goodness," which underlies the proposition that "goodness" is only corrupted by imperfections in the social organizations.

The first and final responsibility for the manner in which each individual uses his life is his own. The non-Conservative submits that the society as a collective entity has a responsibility for individual derelictions. The Conservative asserts that responsibility begins and ends with the individual and that there is no such diffusion on a collective basis. The Conservative accepts as his own the responsibility for the undesirable, unhealthy social conditions that retard and inhibit the moral strengthening of the less favored but rejects the thesis that the responsibility is transferable to the "state" or other collective entity and the individual can thus escape his responsibility to respond to these conditions.

The distinction seems clear. One needs only to examine his own conscience to decide if he believes in the inherent "goodness" of man, which but needs to be liberated from "unhealthy social conditions" to flower in all its richness, or whether one accepts the Conservative view that man's nature is as it is, with a faculty of choice according to his own will.

Once the distinction is accepted and understood, the question remains: how is this tool applied toward influencing the development of society in harmony with the nature of man? Acceptance of the non-Conservative view opens whole areas of "utopian" prospects. The scientific application of intelligence promises to yield a society of abundance where social ills will have disappeared and man's natural goodness is released and given its fullest expression.

The Conservative rejects this view as basically unsound and submits that there is nothing in man's experience to indicate that his nature is anything other than his characteristic individuality. This nature has a capacity for harmony and discord, good and evil, right and wrong, or producing actions in accordance with its own special interest or opposed. Even if the terms of right and wrong are not defined as opposite ends of a moral scale, even if man's nature is considered as capable of infinite choice, it still requires the rejection of the concept of inherent "goodness" and perfectibility.

The acceptance of the Conservative view of mankind compels certain conclusions about the structure of a society in natural harmony. There can be no place of "utopian" ideas calling for a prescribed social structure that by its nature would facilitate the transformation of all into acquiescent, responsive, socially adjusted citizens. It matters not whether some non-Conservative would accept these adjectives as descriptive of the ideal citizen. The point is that the rational, ordered society cannot be relied upon to perfect the nature of man because that nature is not perfectible.

Each individual has a characteristic faculty to choose which response he will make to a given stimulation, and there is no compelling evidence to indicate that this can be transformed by environment. It follows that the form of society that is most in harmony with the nature of man is that society that permits the least restricted exercise of the faculty of choice. In this atmosphere, the maximum human development is facilitated.

The non-Conservative argues that the maximum development will be achieved within the society where the most sophisticated scientific direction is present to encourage and otherwise influence the individual to perform in the general or national interest and therefore his own interest. This would be sort of a benevolent despotism where, as Plato conceived it, philosophers would be kings, or in modern terms, a bureaucracy of non-Conservative elite.

The argument proceeds along the lines that it is the responsibility of the more fortunate and enlightened citizens of the society to provide the "leadership" to the less favored in the pursuit of their best interests. This argument runs into similar difficulties to those Plato encountered. How does society qualify the non-Conservative elite? But this is not the greatest deficiency. The fact of the matter is that man is not this kind of being, and no matter how the non-Conservative tries to fit him to a laboratory mold, man remains what he is in spite of it all.

The faculty to choose freely from among an infinite number of possible responses to a given situation according to the direction of one's own conscience requires exercise to develop. The maximum individual liberty is required to achieve the fullest development. Wherever man is inhibited by institutionalized direction, the need to exercise this faculty of choice is frustrated. Any form of despotism that forces man to conform in behavior to a predetermined pattern compels man to live in an unnatural condition.

The individual does not develop his nature to maturity through a series of habituating exercises as Pavlov's dog. His nature reaches its fullest maturity through the repeated exercise of his will in making the difficult choices presented to him. This is the source of the development of self-discipline where wants and desires are repeatedly subordinated to the demands of responsible and beneficial conduct.

In the absence of liberty, the individual is frustrated. This liberty, however, in no way means license to intrude on the exercise of liberty by fellow men. This is liberty within a disciplined social atmosphere where the fullest measure of liberty possible is secured by operation of law to all.

The question is advanced as to how reliably to secure that maximum measure of liberty to all, consistent with the interests of all. Mechanics, structure, and form become of central significance. Diverse social systems have been devised as a product of man's genius. Some have afforded the individual a substantial measure of liberty to exercise his faculty of choice, and others have almost completely frustrated this through regimentation, intimidation, or inducements. It is in the United States of America, with its political, legal, and social roots deep in Anglo-European tradition, that forms have been developed that most reliably secure this individual condition.

The political institutions of Great Britain, the English-speaking members of the Commonwealth, and those of these united states reveal one impressive common characteristic. The system of law and never the rule of men is the basis of government. The institutions are so contrived that the administration and authority can be passed from hand to hand, and always the institutional form remains strong, reliable, and constant in its guarantees of the rights of the governed. This is the meaning of the rule of law[4] and the "government of the people, by the people, for the people."

The United States has made a unique contribution to and refinement in this system of the rule of law. This is the written Constitution[5]. Whether other parliamentary systems would be strengthened through the formalization of their written constitution is not really relevant. The important point is that the United States Constitution has served the American people well. Who would sleep so well if the guarantees of the Constitution were suddenly subject to repeal by the Congress or to suspension at the whim of the Executive? In the history of the United States, the very liberty of a citizen has often rested finally on this Constitution and liberty has been sustained.

The political institutions of the United States are the source and the embodiment of the order and the virtue of which Burke spoke of when he said, "The only liberty I mean is a liberty connected with order; that not only exists along with order and virtue, but cannot exist at all without them"[6]. The American political institutions are the guardian of the liberties and the reflection of the duties of the citizens of the republic.

When the American Conservative employs his energies in the support of the United States Constitution, the institution of the independent judiciary, the separation of powers, or the Constitutionally reserved powers of the several states, it is the preservation of order and virtue in government that guides his actions; the preservation of that order and virtue without which liberty cannot exist.

Critics have struggled to type the Conservative position as attached to the status quo, that it is characterized by a resistance to change. Some of the non-Conservative pundits have taken a certain delight in referring to Conservatives as eighteenth-century period pieces. If what is meant by adherence to old ideas means a strong attachment to the time-tested ethical standards and the application of ethics to politics, then the Conservative concedes his resistance to change. If this reflects a strong opposition to the erosion of the traditional liberties of the individual and the subjection of the individual to despotism, no matter how benevolent, then he readily admits his resistance to change.

If what is signified is an attachment to political institutions that are those best suited to practical accommodations to constantly changing and developing demands of society, he resists change. If what is meant is that he seeks the preservation of institutions, absolutely subordinate to the system of law, functioning on the principle of inalienable individual rights, then he asserts positively his resistance to change.

The Conservative has a deep attachment to his heritage. He esteems the United States government as the federal and republican form of mechanism that facilitates the orderly development of a free society where each individual may achieve the utmost that lies within his unique capabilities. The Conservative is never insensitive to the fact that a particular institution may have outlasted its usefulness in its prevailing form or that it may be of no use at all. The unreasoned attachment to the past and to tradition solely for the sake of tradition is not a part of the Conservative philosophy.

The Conservative approaches the fact of change from the point of historical perspective. He recognizes that when a particular institution has stood the test of time, trial, and use, and where it has developed over centuries as a safeguard of liberty, it is not to be treated lightly. Never will he carelessly or summarily dismiss the accumulated knowledge and experience of past generations by undermining the Constitution, upsetting the balance of checks built so carefully through the separation of power, the federal system, or sacrifice one single safeguard to the liberty of one individual for some transitory advantage or some apparent gain to the general welfare.[7] The Conservative is acutely conscious of the blood that has been shed, the great sacrifices made over the centuries to yield this land of liberty. He can never relinquish one particle of this liberty for any promise of material well-being or ease.

The Conservative views society as "a partnership in all science; a partnership in all art; a partnership in every virtue, and in all perfection. As the end of such a partnership cannot be obtained in many generations, it becomes a partnership not only between those who are living, but those who are living, those who are dead, and those who are to be born."[8] The objective is the development of a society in which the various forces function to yield an atmosphere facilitating the least restrained development of each individual.

Society is conceived as a living organism, not as a mechanism, a device, a mere social compact. This does not imply that the society has any mystical existence or life apart from the individual members but is in the sense of describing the infinite differences and variations in its composition and the constancy of change in relation to this composition. It is the realization of the infinite possibilities of human accomplishment flowing from the least regulated activity of individuals in pursuit of their own development and that the Conservative reposes his confidence in the fruits of liberty.[9]

Compared to the concepts of Marxian Socialism,[10] with its economic bias and eighteenth—to nineteenth-century stamp and with present-day Liberals with their preoccupation with the "Great Depression"[11], and Keynesian theory,[12] with the oversimplified ideas of social behavior that characterize the political adaptations of the Darwinian[13] theories of evolution and of the Freudian[14] bias in relation to man's controlling drives, where indeed is the answer as to which philosophy favors a dogmatic approach to man's affairs and which position has the greatest capacity to respond to constant change?

THE CONSERVATIVE ESTATE

Whoever will attentively consider the English history, may observe, that the flagrant abuse of any power, by the Crown or its ministers, has always been productive of a struggle which either discovers the exercise of that power to be contrary to law, or (if legal) restrains it for the future.

Whenever the unconstitutional oppressions, even of the sovereign power advance with gigantic strides and threaten desolation of the state, mankind will not be reasoned out of the feelings of humanity, nor will sacrifice their liberty by a scrupulous adherence to those political maxims which were established to preserve it.

—Blackstone

Prudence, indeed, will dictate that governments should not be changed for light and transient causes . . . But when a long train of abuses and usurpations . . . evinces a design to reduce them under absolute despotism, it is their right, it is their duty to throw off such government . . . "

—The Declaration of Independence, July 4, 1776

Time, habit, and repetition have combined to characterize what happened in North America in 1776 as the "American Revolution." This is so particularly among the peoples of the United States. There is an appropriate and emotional attachment to the idea that the men at Philadelphia, at Valley Forge, at Delaware, at Lexington and Concord, and at Yorktown were giving birth not only to a nation but to a revolutionary tradition. Our English brethren do not view it thus. In the long line of English history, this incident is referred to as the "Colonial Rebellion."[15]

Neither the terms *revolution* nor *rebellion* satisfactorily describe the resistance of the North American colonists to the continued rule of the Crown. The consequences of what did transpire are better described as the conservation of a dynamic revolutionary tradition, which grew from the soil of England centuries earlier. The colonists were "conserving" their traditional liberty as Englishmen, from the arbitrary usurpation by George III. Edmund Burke observed at the time:

> The Temper and character, which prevail in our colonies, are, I am afraid, unalterable by any human art. We cannot, I fear, falsify the pedigree of this fierce people, and persuade them that they are not sprung from a nation, in whose being the blood of freedom circulates. The language in which they would hear you tell them this tale, would detect the imposition; your speech would betray you. An Englishman is the unfittest person on earth, to argue another Englishman into slavery.

The American people are heirs of a natural revolutionary tradition, with historical antecedents reaching back through the ages of Western man.[16]

This is a revolution far more exciting in its impact than what happened in the colonies in 1776. There is no desire here to depreciate the significance of the birth of the United States but simply to place this event solidly within the broader revolutionary context. The true revolution is replacement of the rule of men over men by the rule of law, constant and reliable.

The ideas that sparked the rebellion were all associated with the redress of grievances where the colonists thought themselves denied their rights as Englishmen. It was in defense of their inalienable rights that the colonists reluctantly took up arms to defend their traditional liberty from the agents of the King. That Burke approved and defended the actions of the colonists while he stood in horror of the French Revolution is a strong indication of the essentially conservative character of the "American Revolution."

The Federalist Papers comprise one of the most powerful conservative documents of American literature. It was the logic of these writings that persuaded the American people to accept the Constitution. If there remains any lingering doubt as to the essentially conservative character of the origin of this Republic, references need only be made to John Adams's *Defense of the Constitution*; the *Letters of Publicola*, authored by his son, John Quincy Adams; George Washington's *Farewell Address*; and finally, the *Madison Papers*.

The architects of the Constitution conceived of the election of the president by the Electoral College, the Senate by the State legislatures, and the appointment of an independent judiciary as effective checks on popular government. The principles of judicial review by a Supreme Court, whose members are appointed for life and thus immune from popular pressure, were designed to give stability through restraint on Congress. The reservation to Congress of the power to raise revenue was to act as a restraint on the Executive. The objective was to construct a government machinery that was republican in form, where the will of the individual citizen was expressed and given effect through a carefully constructed system of checks and balances that under all circumstances, operated to protect the inalienable rights of the minority.

John Quincy Adams wrote in response to Thomas Paine's *Common Sense*,

> "The eternal and immutable laws of justice and of morality are paramount to all human legislation. The violation of those laws is certainly within the power, but is not among the rights of nations.... It is of infinite consequence that the distinction between power and right should be fully acknowledged as one of the principles of legislators... if a majority... are bound by no law, human or divine, and have no other rule but their sovereign will and pleasure to direct them, what possible security can any citizen of the nation have for the protection of his inalienable rights? The principals of liberty must still be the sport of arbitrary power, and the hideous form of despotism must lay aside the diadem and the scepter, only to assume the party-colored garments of democracy."

Thus, basic distrust of unchecked popular government was a powerful influence in the formation of the particular institutional relationships that are characteristic of our Republic.

On another occasion, Adams observed, "Absolute power intoxicates alike despots, monarchs, aristocrats, and democrats . . ." The objective was to conserve the revolutionary tradition that had seen man gradually free himself from his bondage of thousands of years. It is in this tradition that the American Conservative identifies with the cause of liberty from tyranny.

These are the reasons why he finds in the institutions of the United States forms that work to secure the liberty of the individual and why he works to sustain and nourish these institutional forms. He is reinforced in his conviction by the knowledge that these institutions were carefully fashioned by some of the most profound and imaginative conservative minds mankind has produced.

It is out of this tradition that the Conservative identifies his interests with the interests of mankind to live a life of liberty, where each will be afforded the maximum opportunity to develop his own unique capacities. He recognizes that the defense of the American Constitution is worthy of his greatest and most dedicated effort. Armed with this awareness, he must ask the question, how can this be turned to effective action?

CONSERVATIVE IDENTIFICATION

Consider for a moment the well-intentioned citizen who has devoted his energies to a cause in which he passionately believed only to find that all his work was futile because those who controlled the group were working for a different end. One current example of this is the Communist Front, which traps the well-meaning unwarily into support of apparently humanitarian programs that are used to advance the tyranny of Communism.[17] If the well-meaning individual had been sufficiently discerning, he might have made a more judicious use of his energies and come a good deal closer to the accomplishment of his objective.

A similar problem is often presented to the Conservative, who finds that the only apparatus for the accomplishment of his objective is in the hands of persons who don't share his basic point of view. If the Conservative is to make his efforts count, he must be able to make the distinction between the Conservative and non-Conservative positions. The American non-Conservative position is most frequently encountered in the Liberal.[18]

If there is to be any meaningful distinction between the Liberal and the Conservative, it should lie in the fundamental approaches to human problems. This distinction can be made through use of the concept of "conservation," which forms the durable framework of the Conservative philosophy.

The Conservative takes the world, the universe, and the reality of existence as it is and seeks an individual accommodation that will permit him to live out his life in the greatest harmony with reality. It is this basic acceptance of reality that underlies the whole attitude of conservation. This word *conservation* should be writ large and kept ever before the Conservative consciousness. Never must the Conservative accept substitute attitudes, such as resistance to change, attachment to the status quo, or simply a nostalgic yearning for the "good old days." Conservation is the dynamic and reliable guide. If the Conservative will but test each of his attitudes toward ethical, political, economic, social, or personal question by the test of conservation, he should find that his frame of reference will remain reliably constant.

Should this distinction not be quite clear, a comparative analysis of the fundamental approaches of the various non-Conservative theories with that of the Conservative concept is useful. A reasonably valid generalization is that all non-Conservative systems seek to transform and otherwise revise what is in favor of what their particular bias dictates it ought to be. This attitude is philosophically tagged as "idealism".[19] Frequently, this mantle of idealism is worn when criticizing the Conservative position as not being "idealistic." The implication is that there is something morally reprehensible in not believing that all things lie within the province of man to change and to perfect, even unto his own nature. This concept of idealism is rejected in its entirety.[20] The Conservative is acutely conscious of the full reality of existence and accepts his own individual responsibility to accommodate his own existence with that of his fellow man and all reality.

This does not conflict with a full appreciation of man's capacity to reason and to act reasonably in guiding the use of his faculty of choice. It is in the recognition of the essential reality of this faculty of choice and the very existence of an infinite number of choices that the Conservative differs from his non-Conservative critics.

It is this very reality of the power of reason that logically compels the Conservative to his conclusions. The awareness of this capacity of delayed response to stimuli, to conceive infinity itself, to relate past experiences to present fact, and to anticipate the future lies at the very base of Conservative attitude toward his existence and his responsibilities as a human being. Man is not governed alone by the drives of propagation and survival. Man is never faced with the relatively simple choice of adjusting to his environment to suit his individualistic needs. He has the capacity to employ all the resources of the universe to provide the most suitable environment for the continuing development of his individual capacities.

Man is his own master. He has the capacity to comprehend what is past, apprehend the present, reflect, and contemplate the future. He has the unique capability to so order the utilization of the resources at his disposal as to significantly influence the environment of all generations to come. His capacity to exercise his reason in freely electing between the various choices available to him not only influences his own condition at the time but also has a positive bearing on the condition of his fellow man and that of his children and their children ad infinitum. Man alone has the capacity to use the resources in such a way as to facilitate the constant renewal process. He alone can so direct their employment and the consumption of their fruits so as to conserve the yielding capacity for future generations.

Because of this capacity to apply his intelligence to the conservation of the available resources rather than being relegated to a natural condition where his survival is dependent upon the fleetness of his foot or power of his claw, man alone of all creatures is logically entitled to the fruits of the universe. Accompanying this natural right is the inseparable responsibility to so employ those resources to yield the maximum fruits available to all individuals in order that they may enjoy the fullest development of their own individual capacities. In practice, this means that each has a natural responsibility to conserve all resources at his disposal in such a way that he obtains the maximum utility from them in support of his own and the development of his family members and preserve the remaining utility for the use of his children, his fellow men, and future generations.

The natural and traditional virtues of the Conservative are recognition of the value of work and a dedication to thrift and husbandry.[21] These virtues are the essential qualities that impart vigor and force to the entire concept of conservation. The Conservative embraces these virtues out of an appreciation of the ever-expanding requirements of man. He recognizes that the very progress of mankind out of the ooze has been grounded in the accumulated product of all who had been born, lived, struggled, and perished before him. Western man stands tall today only because he stands atop the broad shoulders of all who preceded him. He cannot deny such support to his children.

Perhaps at no other time in the dynamic development of the American Conservative position has there been a greater need for these virtues than now when so many primitive peoples are struggling to arise above the level of bare subsistence and man is at the same time reaching for the stars. At no other time have resources been so in need of careful husbandry. Make no mistake; we are not affluent; resources are scarce when measured against the needs they must serve. The universe is bountiful, but it will take dedicated work and all man's genius to so employ these resources so that there will be abundance for all.

ANATOMY OF LIBERTY AND PROPERTY

Recognition of the value of work is one of the essential virtues that impart vigor and force to the entire concept of conservation. This does not mean that the Conservative is attached to any therapeutic idea of work for work's sake. He does not believe that man works as a natural and virtuous condition simply for the sake of performing some combination of mental and physical tasks. Man works to acquire property. He is motivated by a need to gain some element of control over the fruits of his labor.

As a general principle, whether man is self-employed or hires out his skills to another, his object is to realize a return in the form of an accumulation of property. He expects to obtain possession of this property and to have the right to dispose of it as he sees fit. When this phrase, *obtain possession* is used, it should be equated with *command possession*. This follows from the nature of a money economy where the worker is most often compensated for labor in monetary units. If the equation is to be exact, monetary units must be convertible into equivalent property at the will of the holder.

This understanding of the relationship of property to work leads to the logical appreciation of the institution of the private ownership of property as a fundamental part of the Conservative structure. Because of the very fundamental nature of this institution, it has been subject to the heaviest non-Conservative assaults. Leaning heavily upon the abundant evidence of man's corrupt use of the institution to serve his perverse ends, critics have sought to discredit the validity of the institution itself.[22]

The transparent fallacies in their logic have not lessened their emotional appeal to those who have been without property and have found themselves abused by those who have property and have used it irresponsibly. This problem of reconciling the right to ownership of property resident in the individual, with the responsibility to the family, to the community, and to future generations, has occupied the attention of all who have accepted the defense of the institution.

In the European feudal society, a certain level of reconciliation was achieved through a whole system of rights and responsibilities where the lord and the serf mutually supported each other and defended each other's interest.[23] With the decline of feudal society accompanied by the centralization of the government under the monarchy, it was in the interest of the king to further weaken the bonds between the lord and the serf.

The lords were seduced to leave their vast estates and to take up residence in the court. Their privileges were increased as their responsibilities were removed to be assumed by the central government. It is little wonder that the landed aristocracy became so vulnerable to the egalitarian revolutions, which swept across Europe. France in 1789 is the classic example of the condition of vulnerability where the ownership of the property was substantially in absentia, accompanied by great privilege without commensurate responsibilities.[24]

What can be said of France in 1789 takes on increased emphasis when considering Imperial Russia of 1917. There, the institution of private property was vulnerable for much the same reasons as France of 1789. True enough, the consequence of the French Revolution was not complete destruction of the institution as later was the case in Russia, but this should be attributed to the events surrounding and following the convulsion and not underlying it. In Russia, when the propertied aristocracy was swept away, there was in existence a highly developed social theory in the hands of a militant force to bring about the complete destruction of the institution.

The Conservative does not believe that what happened in France and later in Russia was an indictment of the validity of the institution but is evidence that the institution can become vulnerable under conditions where there is a great concentration of property in the hands of a restricted number of individuals, resulting in the consequent great disparity of distribution. This vulnerability is accented by the irresponsible administration of the property in the hands of the owners.

The non-Conservative asks the question, "How can he (the Conservative) profess to be a realist, to take life on its own terms, as it were, and at the same time reject the evidence that private ownership of property inevitable leads to concentration in the hands of individuals who abuse the ownership and thus bring about its (the institution's) vulnerability?"

The answer to be understood is that the Conservative recognizes that the institution can become vulnerable to devastating attack where it is badly administered, but this is a weakness of all institutions and in no way goes to the root of essential validity. The root question to be raised is whether the private ownership of property corresponds to the nature of man and thus is a natural condition. The Conservative believes that the answer to this question is in the affirmative; thus, the conservation of the institution is requisite to the further development of society that will facilitate the unobstructed development of the individual.

Man has not always lived in a highly sophisticated society characterized by complex control (governmental, business, finance, etc.) mechanisms. Substantial evidence indicates that the mechanism's very complexity has had a direct relationship to population density and developing technology. As man's numbers have grown, as his technology advanced and as his knowledge has become more profound, he has steadily sought a closer relationship with his fellow man. The reasons for this are many, complex, and interrelated. We need not consider them in detail here.[25] It is sufficient that this is so and that it has led to a fuller life for each individual to support the thesis that society has certain attributes worth conserving.

Little imagination is required to call forth the picture of primitive man existing in the wilderness with limited command over his environment, subject to the intrusion of every marauding beast. The greater portion of his earliest existence must have been devoted to subduing his physical surroundings and defending his person and those of his family from violent attack. The development of his essentially human character was severely limited by virtue of the little time available for its cultivation. How could he store up much knowledge when each moment of his existence was devoted to the one controlling activity, survival?

When man discovered the fertility of the soil and, as a consequence, gave up his nomadic existence of hunt for the stay-at-home life of the farm, he put down roots and acquired property. He acquired property[26] in the land and in the implements that his ingenuity produced to cultivate the land. As man acquired property in the land through his toil, the result was to free him from many of the uncertainties of raw nature and to place himself increasingly in command of his environment. He discovered early on that his family was a source of strength in this new life, and he found in association with his fellow man that this strength could be multiplied.

As man grouped together, he perceived that he must yield some of his individualistic ways for the benefit of the society so that essential liberty could be preserved. This did not mean that man enjoyed a greater measure of liberty in the relative isolation of his primeval condition. In the beginning, liberty was closely circumscribed by the very fact that he faced a forbidding and grudging environment with none save his own resourcefulness to sustain him. Here was born the realization by each individual member of the social group of the necessity to act with restraint that each may enjoy his full measure of liberty in harmony with each other. When this fact was recognized, social order was born of the creature of the rule of law.[27]

From the earliest times, the law has accorded some recognition of a right in each individual to the product of his toil and labor. This point is illustrated by reference to the fifth book of Moses, Deuteronomy 1:21: "Behold, the Lord thy God hath set forth the land before thee; go up and possess it." This is reinforced by reference to book 5, verse 21: "Neither shall thou desire thy neighbor's wife; neither shalt thou covet thy neighbor's house, his field, or his manservant, his ox, or his ass or anything that is thy neighbor's." This reference is not introduced to invoke a divine authority to sustain the Conservative position. This is the province of the theologians. The purpose is to illustrate that the right to ownership was recognized in our antiquity and the exercise of that right had the sanction of law from the earliest days.

There is a great wealth of historical evidence upon which to draw in evaluation of the significance of the institution of the private ownership of property[28] to the security of individual liberty. The entire history of our people as they sought to subdue a savage land is filled with evidence of the pioneer who went into virtual isolation and possessed the land. The stories of these rugged and courageous men and women who sought liberty to grow and achieve the fullest development of their unique capabilities excite the imagination of all Americans. That they encountered a forbidding environment is clear. That they found it desirable to group together in settlements under a system of law is equally clear from the "Mayflower Compact," through the institution of the "wagon boss," the "frontier marshal," and the "vigilantes," and it is just as certain that each of these systems was found wanting because of the susceptibility to subversion by men. In all instances, the law was called upon to give effect to society's recognition of the right of each man to the possession and unrestricted right of disposition of the product of his labor. That the operation of the systems was imperfect is certain, but it is equally certain that the society recognized a property right in the individual, which it was in the interest of all to sustain and protect.

Should the inseparability of the condition of liberty and the right to own property remain obscure, consider the plight of those who are denied the ownership. These are dependent human beings through all the days of their existence. Their natural liberty is stripped from them by their "benefactors," upon whose bounty they depend for subsistence. Look upon the miserable condition of the unfree people[29] under Communist dictatorships. Even the most articulate apologists of Communism can no longer hide the degradation of the humanity that is ground down in a steady dehumanizing process under the weight of the monolithic Communist state. In its most brutal form, the Communist regime of China, commune regimentation, seeks to dehumanize humanity and cultivate a "Communist Citizen" in its place. The hideous example of Communism simply illustrates the extent to which the dehumanizing process is susceptible when the right of the ownership of property is usurped from the individual by the state.

The Conservative affirms without qualification the right to the private ownership of property; furthermore, he emphasizes the necessity of minimum restrictions of disposition right where the restrictions on disposition materially interfere with the use of the property as the owner sees fit. Minimum restrictions of use are those restrictions that are required so that the use will not materially infringe upon the right of others to use and enjoy their property.

Traditionally, these restrictions have been implemented through the exercise of the "police power" of the state. The principles that guide this use of state police power involve the concepts of public safety, public health, or public welfare.

Reference to judicial opinion reveals a wide difference of concept among jurists as to what is meant by safety, health, and welfare. The Conservative does not pretend to support a general synthesis or consensus on the point. He does have certain traditional ideas that correspond to his basic positions.

Safety here means that degree of protection required to give reasonable insurance that each individual enjoys the liberty of his person from interference by another person through the perpetration of a criminal act, a negligent act, of the negligent failure to act where there was a duty to act. Safety does not mean a social guarantee from the normal hazards of living, which so limit conduct as to materially restrict liberty. The Conservative accepts the fact that the very act of living entails certain risks to the person and that the very nature of life demands that the individual, participating to the limit of his capabilities, must be exposed to these risks. It lies within the judgment of the individual to so govern his own conduct as to compensate for the risks.

This matter of the relationship of public safety and individual liberty may be understood in terms of traffic regulation. It certainly is possible to introduce sufficient regulation into the operation of a motor vehicle that the risk of injury would be negligible. For example, all traffic could be required to proceed at speeds under twenty miles per hour. Licensing of vehicles could be restricted to only those that incorporated the maximum of mechanical safety feature, and the privilege of driving could be limited to a very few highly qualified drivers.

Ridiculous, one might say. The point is that it is theoretically possible for the state to employ the police power to so limit the conduct of the citizens as to effectively remove the practical possibility of an injury arising from the operation of a motor vehicle. The Conservative rejects this approach as an unacceptable use of the police power. It would constitute an unreasonable intrusion into the essential liberty of the individual. Liberty is much too precious to be sacrificed to a super abundance of caution designed to provide guarantees to those who flee from the natural hazards of living in close proximity with their fellow man. The problem is ever one of balancing the interest to be protected against the liberty to be preserved, and the emphasis is always on liberty.

The matter of health doesn't present quite the difficulties associated with the conflict between the "public interest" and individual liberty as does safety, but the possibility of conflict exists even here. Here, the state is concerned with the matter of contagion, and the fact that one citizen might use his property in a way that breeds disease that would be no respecter of property lines. The Conservative has few reservations concerning the use of the police power to require that each property owner use his property so as to avoid pollution of the waters, the atmosphere, or the land. As an example of Conservative reservations in this area, however, method is worth considering. It would be clearly contrary to basic Conservative principles to approve the suspension of the constitutionally guaranteed freedom from unwarranted search and seizure simply to make the job of the Public Health official easier.[30]

Much greater difficulty is encountered in this area when persons of pronounced eccentricities are confined against their will in the interests of the public health. Here, only the clearest demonstration of the danger would satisfy the Conservative that confinement with its complete loss of liberty is justified. The Conservative is hard-pressed to even acquiesce to measures that require the citizen to take certain measures that the state believes beneficial to his health. The matter of the state adulterating the water supply under the theory that the ingestion of the chemicals is healthful seems wholly beyond the legitimate exercise of police power.

This reluctance to support and frequent active opposition to activities by the state to "promote the public health" exposes the Conservative to much criticism as being insensitive to matters of the health of the people. In answer, he must rely on his attachment to the principle of individual liberty and to explain his opposition to compulsory polio vaccination or state fluoridation of the water supply as being beyond the legitimate exercise of the police power. To do so would be an unwarranted invasion of the liberty of the individual to guard his health as he sees fit.

If distinctions must be drawn, then it might be made between the enforced vaccination of an entire population against a disease that clearly threatened epidemic proportions and the enforced inoculation against routine possibility of infection. The line might also lie somewhere between the chlorination of the water supply for purposes of purification and the enforced fluoridation to guard against another source of infection and decay. A useful thought might be that if the liberty of the citizen is to be sustained, he must retain the right to guard his own health as he sees fit except where his failure to do so carries the clear danger of contamination to his fellow citizens.

In the area of "welfare," the Conservative encounters the most persistent and direct conflict with the non-Conservative. This does not mean that the Conservative resists more vigorously the tendency to intrude on individual liberty under the guise of promoting the "public welfare" than where the intrusion is under the cover of health or safety. It is simply that the whole concept of employing the coercive power of the state to guard and promote the public welfare is saturated with dangers of abuse, usurpation of authority, and illegitimate exercise of power.

For example, where this power is employed to provide for the children who are the victims of parental neglect, there seems little basis for objection on the grounds of reduced liberty. But where this power intrudes so far into the lives of the citizens as to actually encourage the condition it seeks to relieve, the Conservative must object. Where the system of welfare so reduces the citizen to a level of dependency as to rob him of all dignity, this is enslavement regardless of how well intentioned the act.

Objections become increasingly clear where we witness the unhappy picture of the state actually encouraging promiscuity and illegitimate birth through subsistence payments to the natural mother so long as she cares for the illegitimate child. If this policy is not calculated to achieve a degradation of the human spirit on a compound basis, then the proponents are blind to the product.

The non-Conservative argues that the child is better off with the natural mother. Since she must care for the child without the benefit of the father, society must accept the burden. This argument completely ignores the fact that frequently the child, so raised by a woman of easy virtue, is raised in the most demoralizing atmosphere possible, where the child's only value to the mother is the subsistence check.[31]

This does not mean, of course, that the Conservative does not recognize some legitimate state activities in guarding and even promoting the public welfare. The child labor laws are an excellent example. Here, the basic difficulty to overcome in enacting such a law was the problem of reconciling this with the liberty of the individual to contract his service to another and the legal protection of contract rights. When considering this matter, it is important to keep always in mind the significance to our society of the principle that a promise freely given for some consideration, such as another promise, money, or a service, is enforceable in a court of law against the giver of the promise. Think of the disorder and the uncertainties that would exist in our lives if this were not so.

It is just this specter of social chaos that loomed so large in the minds of those who first considered the child labor laws. To pretend that they were insensitive to the undesirable social conditions that saw small children at the looms during long hours when they should be home having their minds and bodies nourished is to approach the ridiculous. The social pressure was great, the objections were swept away, and the laws prohibiting the employment of persons under a certain age in certain occupations were enacted.[32]

Compulsory education laws were also enacted to ensure that the children who now could not work would be profitably occupied in education. Consider now the product as large numbers of young hoodlums and youthful derelicts roam the streets as wolves contemptuous of all authority except "the leader." Why are so many young children unoccupied? The answer is obvious. They are unable to continue in the compulsory school system, and they are prohibited from working. The immense energies of their youth will find an outlet in lawlessness and dereliction. What does the non-Conservative tell us? More case workers and a bigger welfare budget because the case load has increased. This is the unremitting dogmatic pronouncement flowing from social-welfare doctrine.

How would the Conservative approach this problem? First of all, he would seek to avoid rigid social patterns wherever possible. The objective would be to deal with the detrimental aspects of child labor without relegating the child to idleness. The answer, of course, is not to assign the child who can no longer profit from continued academic schooling to a "youth club" so that his hours are consumed in play. "All work and no play" may make "Jack a dull boy," but all play and no work will guarantee he will become a troublesome nothing.

Traditionally, all minor children are the wards of our courts. In theory, this means that the impartial magistrate is interested in the welfare of the youth. If the judge determines that the unoccupied minor child should be gainfully employed, what sense does it make to prohibit this possibility to the judge who is considering the individual case? It lies safely within the province of judicial wisdom to guard the real interests of our youth. The final discretion would be placed where it belongs in the court, and nothing would be prohibited in discharging the responsibility to guard the opportunities of our youth to achieve their fullest development.

The whole matter of welfare reaches frightening proportions when we witness the federal government bureaucracy deciding what should be planted, how much, what price it should bring, whose money should be taken and redistributed to whom, where citizens should live, in what kind of homes, in what neighborhoods, how much they should work, who they should hire, who they can fire, who shall go to what school, how much employees will be paid, what price the seller will charge for his property, how citizens will provide for their declining years, and how much property will be taken through planned inflation, to be distributed to what favored group.

The picture presented of the federal government under the direction of the non-Conservative is somewhat similar to a man running between two platforms on a scale. As the man stands on one platform and surveys the other, he sees the opposite platform begin to rise. Driven by this compulsion toward planned equilibrium, he notes the amount of weight needed to restore the balance, seizes this weight, and leaps from his platform, and races toward the other. He heaves the required weight onto the rising platform and climbs aboard as he views with satisfaction that the platform begins to fall. He then looks back at the platform from whence he came in horror. Now he sees it begin to rise. He repeats the process without interruption, always in quest of planned stability, never once realizing that it is his own weight constantly moving back and forth that causes the recurring crises.

The only way to approach this matter of welfare is to consider on its merits each instance where the power of the state is to be employed to guard or promote the general or public welfare. The Conservative insists that the welfare involved be really general or public in character. In practice, it is not a legitimate activity of the state to use its power on behalf of one particular group of citizens against another under the guise of promoting the general or public welfare.

It is not a legitimate function of government to line up with all antique pewter dealers to "redress an economic imbalance" in favor of stainless steel cookery manufacturers. It is not a legitimate function of government to tax the merchants on Seventh Avenue in order to subsidize the older merchants on Eighth Avenue who have lost business to the newer neighborhoods. It is not a legitimate function of government to tax the citizens of Industrial City, Michigan, in order to subsidize the "depressed" residents of Uranium City, Colorado, after the ore has run out.

Imagine the miserable social conditions that could have been perpetuated by a benevolent welfare system armed with the "depressed area" concept when the gold of California began to run out of the gold fields.

What red-blooded American lacks a sentimental attachment to the "village smithy" at his forge? The smith and his apprentice son are part of the finer traditions of frontier America. The family-operated forge that was ever ready to shoe an unshod horse, day or night, was essential to the "American way of life." The immensity of the program, which could have developed when the automobile began to replace the horse as the common method of transport power, staggers the imagination. Great stretches of our unused plains could have been reserved to graze unneeded horses, hundreds of displaced wranglers could have been employed, and thousands of family forges could have been preserved.

It may not be really safe to venture beyond the point of recognizing in each citizen the right to the quiet enjoyment of his property rights and to the exercise of his inalienable rights undisturbed by the actions of his neighbor. When domestic tranquility is threatened by interference, the power of the state is appropriately invoked to prevent the threatened or real abuse. This always relates to the preservation of an established right and never to the acquisition of an advantage over another.

In essence, the Conservative's concern is with the liberty of the individual. He is persuaded that the institution of the private ownership of property is inseparable from the fact of liberty. The right of ownership carries with it the indispensable right to use and dispose of the property as the owner sees fit. This right is only limited by the legitimate exercise of the state "police power" to ensure that the use does not deprive another of the free use and disposition of his property.

That there will inevitably be conflicting interests and interferences and transgressions by one against the rights of another are accepted. First reliance is upon the application of the remedies under the law rather than prior restraint to redress the wrong. Resort to prior restraint is had only where the wrong could not be set right through legal remedies, such as damages. The American Conservative has a strong attachment to the common-law system of a specific remedy to redress a specific wrong. He is extremely reluctant to employ the remedy of prior restraint, either judicial or administrative, except where there is no remedy for the probable wrong, or where the legal remedy is clearly not adequate to redress the injury.

Up to this point, we have considered the matter of right of private ownership relating to the individual. That this right and its free exercise are fundamental to the condition of individual liberty is accepted. A single consideration of the man who is denied the right and his consequent total dependency status is enough. That the enjoyment of this right is a natural condition arising out of the nature of man is apparent from man's natural obligations to his family.

Man in the society of his fellow man has certain obligations that naturally arise out of the association. The primary obligations are those that attach by virtue of his family relationships. These comprise the whole body of his domestic responsibilities. They involve such things as providing for the education of his children, feeding and clothing his dependents, and caring for aged and needy parents. These obligations issue directly from the marital relationship. This is an ancient institution, older than the state itself.[33]

The biological nature of the male as distinguished from the female has cast the male in the role as provider. As a natural corollary to this role, the male occupies a position of authority as head of the household.

There is no implication here that paternal authority is other than parental in nature. It does not exist separate from the authority of both the father and the mother over the offspring. The wife's title and authority are co-equal but not quite identical. The children are bound to both parents in the sense that commanding their obedience as "honor thy father and thy mother" (Exodus 20:12) and "children, obey your parents" (Ephesians 6:1).

The salient point is that in this capacity of provider, the father has had the responsibility to provide for the sustenance of the family and the resources necessary to support their development. It is the responsibility of the father to provide each of his children with opportunity and guidance such that the child will be prepared to accept his responsibilities upon reaching maturity.

In no other way can these family responsibilities be discharged except that the individual has the right to acquire property and to apply this property as he sees fit to satisfy his and his family's needs.

Inseparable from the right to the ownership of property is the right to the benefits from the ownership. This means a protected right to the rents, the issues, and the profits from the ownership, the use, and the disposition of the property. As the right of ownership would be a barren right without the accompanying right of use, so it would be deprived of all force in supporting individual liberty if the owner were to be denied the benefits issuing therefrom. To withdraw the benefits of use would have the effect of discouraging the use and encouraging the retention of the property in idleness. This would result in the negation of one of the basic Conservative principles: to encourage the maximum employment of resources for productive purposes.

The productive use of resources is the means by which additional disposable resources are generated and become available for distribution to individual ownership. Recognizing that the right of ownership of property is indispensable to the realization of a condition of individual liberty and recognizing that the individual enjoyment of this right is the means by which the individual secures to himself this condition of liberty, the Conservative believes that the state, through the system of law, has a legitimate responsibility to encourage the widest possible diffusion and ownership of property interests. The basis for the realization of this condition of wide diffusion is abundance, for it is through the generation of the maximum property available to ownership that the opportunities for ownership are maximized.

Not only does the right to the enjoyment of the fruits of ownership secure the liberty of the individual, but also it positively encourages the use in such a manner as to increase the total wealth available for distribution of ownership and thereby contributes to an ever-widening realization of the fullest condition of liberty. In this way, it can be fairly stated that another principle of the Conservative is to encourage the widest possible diffusion of the private ownership of property.

There is an old American saying to the effect that "the rich get richer and the poor get poorer." Even the more biased views of American history over the past fifty years would force denial of the validity of the whole of this correlation. The poor have certainly not become poorer. They have, in fact, become more prosperous. However, the other end of the folk saying would probably prove fairly accurate. The rich do tend to get richer, or perhaps more accurately, the ownership of property tends to generate the further accumulation of property. We can only say "tends" because it is equally apparent that the unsuccessful management will lead to the diminution of the ownership.

Given the case that private ownership of property is fundamental to the realization of the condition of liberty, is it not valid to view with a certain amount of suspicion, a system that permits, even facilitates, increasing accumulations? If dependency is the denial of liberty in the dependent, then is not relative dependence a relative denial of such liberty? If the natural operation of the system facilitates, even encourages, a relative disparity in the accumulation of property, does not the system itself tend toward a relative denial of liberty to the less favored? These three questions are of critical significance and demand satisfactory answers. This is so if the institution of the private ownership of property is to be validly associated with the Conservative position or simply a defense of vested interest.

The answer to the first question is an unqualified yes. The Conservative will always view this system and any other for that matter with definite suspicion. Systems tend to become institutionalized, and institutions tend toward the development of a hierarchy of power. The hierarchy of power, or power elite, tends to develop vested interests and become preoccupied with the problems and the techniques of power and, as such, become less reliable custodians of the power they wield, less reliable in the sense of contributing to the healthy operation of the system. The Conservative finds much truth in the observation of Lord Acton: "Power corrupts and absolute power corrupts absolutely."

The second question is answered with a qualified no. While it is true that dependency is a denial of liberty in the dependent and relative dependence a relative denial, there is a point of diminishing applicability to this observation. From the point of relative accumulations of property and the accompanying economic power as relates to individual liberty, the relative correlation operates within very broad limits.

This point may be expressed through the use of an analogy despite the obvious weaknesses of analogical exposition. In gross comparison, certainly the dependency for caviar does not have the same impact as the dependency for bread. Even considering the relative abundance of our society, the fact that one person may be able to command a Chevrolet automobile once every five years has very little relationship to his relative liberty as compared to the person who commands a new Lincoln or Rolls-Royce, for that matter, every year. The central point is that after the individual has command of sufficient property to support himself and his family according to their basic needs with a reasonable degree of independence, the fact that he is relatively dependent for further accumulations has a sharply diminishing relationship to his liberty quotient.

The answer to the third question is an unqualified no. The system tends toward the opposite condition. The natural operation of the system tends toward the realization of liberty by the less favored. The very accumulation of property in the hands of those who have successfully competed for its ownership, within the marketplace economy, is the most reliable assurance that the property will move into the strongest economic hands. The consequence is that concentrations of property will be in the hands of those individuals who have demonstrated the greatest ability to employ the property productively. By rising to positions of economic power, these individuals will have demonstrated a capacity to utilize the resources their position of power commands in the most efficient, effective, and productive manner. For these reasons, they are demonstrably the most reliable custodians of the great economic power that accompanies large property accumulations.

If the individual of limited competitive capabilities, less favored as it were, is to have a reasonable expectation of securing to himself the condition of liberty that property ownership and economic independence brings, he must rely upon abundance to make the acquisition of the property relatively easy. It is in his direct interest, therefore, that the greater accumulations of productive resources available are in the directive hands of those individuals of the highest degree of demonstrated productive capabilities.

Critics of the marketplace economy and the selection system, which operates to secure economic power, have characterized it as a blind system incapable of yielding the result we have just cited with an acceptable degree of consistency. To illustrate the criticism, they cite example after example of demonstrated inability in the custodians of large property accumulations. Not without accuracy, it is pointed out that many have arrived at their propertied state through inheritance, paternalistic favor, political intrigue, or some other economically noncompetitive mechanism or technique. The answer is that this system is imperfect and capable of being subverted by man, as is any system, the system of justice, for example.

As blindness is a virtue in the system of justice, so blind selection in the economic system is a virtue. Absolute economic benefits cannot reasonably be expected any more than absolute justice. Equal economic opportunity is the condition fundamental to economic justice and is the very companion to equality before the law.[34] This is the sense of it—liberty inheres in the sensible object.

As the Conservative relies upon the system of equity[35] to meliorate the sometimes-harsh application of the common-law system, so he relies on a variety of meliorating devices to compensate for the sometimes-harsh workings of the marketplace system. As the need for equity in no way invalidates the demonstrated utility of the impersonal system of law, so the need for moderating devices in no way invalidates the demonstrated utility of the marketplace. The Conservative places the same type of reliance upon the public, exercising its right of free choice within the marketplace to be the most reliable judge of economic fact, as he does upon the jury of citizen peers in the court of law. Similarly, as he relies upon the wisdom of the independent judiciary, he relies upon the functioning of a professional hierarchy of economic arbiters within the independent agencies to be the interpreters of the economic rules. Where the workings of the marketplace fail to provide substantial economic justice, he relies upon the operation of the economic equity agencies to meliorate the system. Reliance upon the integrity of the responsible custodians of law and finance or banking is fundamental to the Conservative position.

It is demonstrable that the intrusion of the Executive in the functionings of the independent Judiciary on a partisan basis will inevitably lead to the subversion of substantial justice in favor of partisan advantage and special privilege. This same observation applies to the intrusion of the government into the functioning of the marketplace economy through either attempting to dictate the fact determination of the consumer and the judgment of the Federal Reserve System[36] or influence the actions of the special agencies.

Typical examples of non-Conservative actions in the subversion of substantial economic justice in favor of partisan advantage and special privilege are represented by price, rent, and wage controls, economic subsidies, resource allocation, manipulation of the money supply through monetization of the public debt by political influence over the operations of the Federal Reserve System, and perhaps the grossest example of all is the boldness with which the National Labor Relations Board is treated as a partisan agency. The popularly elected Executive is no more the reliable custodian of directive economic power than he would be the reliable custodian of judicial power or authority to direct the religious life of the nation.

The growth of powerful concentrations of economic power that have a disruptive effect on constructive competition has been a characteristic of the American society. Monopoly or near monopoly power is contrary to Conservative principles regardless of form. The existence of the monopoly has the effect to lessen the impact of the forces that work in the free competitive market to encourage maximum productive application of the resources available. Just as the "price of liberty is eternal vigilance," so too is the price of effective and free economic competition. As the monopoly most frequently arises out of a subversion of the competitive market through an alliance with political power to insulate the monopoly from the action of the market, the Conservative remedy is to divorce the political-economic marriage and to effectively remove the monopoly from the sheltering arms of government, thereby exposing it to the rigors of competition.

Not all monopolies or near-monopoly combinations in restraint of free competition, however, arise out of a marriage between political and economic power. Some simply arise out of the particular functioning of the marketplace itself where time and site factors combine to give a peculiar advantage to a certain economic concentration. The reward for highly successful competition is to run every competitor out of business; thus, the monopoly results substantially by default.

The Conservative does not rely on prior limitations to the accumulation and the use of property to remove the dangers of monopoly combinations. It is through the vigorous, nonpartisan prosecution of the laws relating to illegal combinations and conspiracies in restraint of trade that the Conservative achieves a fluid equilibrium in power distribution facilitating the constructive operation of the marketplace. He conceives of the role of the state not as a limiting authority controlling the accumulation and use of economic power but as an agency providing for redress or restraint where the interests of others have been injured or are threatened with irreparable harm.

One of the unique features of American economic history has been the growth of the corporate form of property ownership. When the courts accorded the corporation the status of a legal person with all of the rights to own, use, and receive the fruits of property, accompanied by the recognition of the liability limitations to the equity owners, a decisive step was taken away from the individual enterprise that had dominated the American economy. Neither the Sherman Antitrust Act of 1890 nor the

Clayton Act of 1914 seemed to have any limiting effect on the development of the corporation as the characteristic form of great and concentrated property accumulation.

The Conservative is in full agreement with the philosophy of the Sherman and Clayton acts as they rule in favor of economic competition. This does not mean, however, that the Conservative can approve of these particular laws and their application. Under the administration of both acts, there has been a disturbing tendency to judge criminality after the fact in a manner that can only be accurately described as ex post facto. This has constituted a sacrifice of a major constitutional protection and is thus totally unacceptable.

It is from this position in favor of economic competition that the Conservative views the special problems presented by the corporation. One of the most critical problems has to do with the relationship of profit to competition. The laissez-faire economist had assumed that the impulse to maximize profit within the marketplace economy was the guarantor of continued competition. The theory was that under conditions of "perfect competition," as the profits increased to one or a limited number of producers, others would be induced to enter this line of business; thus, there would be a kind of freely oscillating adjustment of production to meet the effective demand. The critics of the laissez-faire position, besides making the obvious observation that "perfect competition" never exists, cite the growth of the corporate form, with accompanying decline of individual enterprise, as evidence discrediting the marketplace as a control mechanism.

The point is that the directive control of the corporation is not in the exclusive hands of the stockholders who can be assumed to be motivated by the prospects of profit. More often with the larger corporations, the directive control is in the hands of a professional management, which is not under the exclusive control of the stockholders, so far as the motivation to maximize profits is concerned. The usual institutional motives of vested interest, power acquisition, prestige, community acceptance, and ease of management itself are clearly some of the motives that influence the direction of corporate enterprise, where the managers are not primarily affected by profit.

What is, in fact, recognized is that many modern corporate managers are in a position to set their own rates of compensation through the use of their companion positions as directors. The result is that the director-manager's take-home pay may have little relationship to the productive way he uses the resources of the business and a great relationship to the success he has in mastering the techniques of power to support his position within the corporate hierarchy. The larger the corporation and the more widely held the equity ownership, the less direct control the owners have over the conduct of the management, and thus, theoretically, the less motivated by profit maximization will the management be.

The Conservative does not pretend that profit alone is the motivation that guides the modern corporate manager in his management decisions any more than he ever accepted the laissez-faire justification of perfect competition to validate the marketplace mechanism. As the Conservative looks upon the whole of human society as an organism where the myriad of internal and external factors function in an interrelated manner to produce a functioning equilibrium facilitating constructive development, he looks upon the economy as an organic component of the organic society.

The corporate manager is motivated in his decisions by a complex interaction of economic gain or profit, personal position or prestige, social or community acceptance and approval, etc. No matter how far removed or insulated from effective control of the equity owners, the manager remains primarily motivated by the requirement to sustain the economic health of the business.

The enterprise will be administered in such a way that the interests of all those individuals who are associated with the business will be served. Profits will have to be adequate to attract equity financing; the financial position will have to be sound to qualify for the loan of capital; prices and quality will have to remain competitive to command the market; and the requirements of the employees for their share of the gross will have to be met according to their productivity. Where the productivity is high, the resistance to compensation increases is low, and the reverse is the case where the productivity is low.

The fact of entitlement to a share in the productivity increase by the employee arises from a retention of earnings as part of the capital accumulation available for modernization and development. Of course, a share must go to the equity owners for a similar reason; and a portion, to management to reflect the part attributable to the improved management techniques and performance.

The regulation of business enterprise is reluctantly accepted as necessary where it is required to maintain equilibrium of economic interest. The disruption of the equilibrium comes about where a particular business functions in an economic atmosphere of sharply reduced competition. The necessity to resort to governmental regulation arises where it is either impossible or socially undesirable to resort to the antimonopoly or anticombination devices to create or restore the atmosphere of competition.

The Conservative first relies upon the workings of the free competitive market to achieve the most productive use of the available resources. The confidence in the market is based upon a conviction that this will yield the maximum abundance available to ownership to all, and in this way, the interests of liberty will be served. Governmental regulation is accepted warily, with great hesitancy, and is subjected to a continuing review in order that the elimination of the regulation will follow as closely as possible upon the disappearance of the need.

Where the need rests upon an absence of effective competition, the basis for regulation disappears with the restoration of competition. Needs do not generally disappear instantaneously, and during the period of time that competition is being restored, the regulatory agency characteristically will find a variety of other reasons to sustain its vested interest. The fact that this is a natural bureaucratic and institutional phenomenon in no way validates the reasons so developed. The rather painful readjustment must be made regardless of the complex control mechanisms devised.

The current conditions of the American railroads in particular, and the transportation industry in general, is an excellent case in point. Here, the regulation has been carried far beyond the needs of the public and has lasted long after sufficient competition has existed within the industry to ensure that the substantial public interest would be better served by the operations of the competitive market. The fact that the management of the regulatory agency, the management of the railroads, and the management of the labor unions concur in their resistance of deregulation in no way sustains the case for continued regulation. All should be suspect of having developed over the years an institutionalized vested interest in continued regulation and that this accounts for their reluctance to be now exposed to the risks of competition.

Unequal accumulations of property will naturally flow from the operation of a free competitive economy. This follows from the fact that individuals are unequal competitors. The Conservative recognizes that men are not in fact the same, that each individual is unique, having a unique combination of capabilities that contribute to his particular individual development. This richness of diversity has been at once the catalytic agent and the substance of civilization. When these unique capabilities are applied within the scope of economics, the natural consequence is unequal accumulation of property.

The Conservative does not resist this fact but conversely views it as another evidence of a unique specialization of talent. He knows that to burden a Rembrandt with the property sustained by a Ford could not only lead to a condition of no automobiles but also, more tragically, no paintings.

Consider the condition of the cobbler, the merchant who sells the shoes, and the manufacturer who directs the production. It makes only good sense to support the system that puts the tools in the hands of the craftsman, the merchandise in the hands of the merchant, and the resources in the hands of the organizer-producer. The result, of course, is to facilitate the quantitatively unequal accumulation of property, but anything else would simply overburden or frustrate the individual and thus prevent him from realizing his fullest personal development and related contribution. The man who has demonstrated an organizational and directive talent to make the most productive use of resources should not be denied the resources to give expression to his unique capacities to serve his and, consequently, the interest of others to the maximum. This same principle applies to the woodman and his ax, the writer and his pen, and the machine operator and his machine.

The Conservative does not hold one productive talent in higher esteem than another. Artist, banker, laborer, craftsman, manager, framer—all occupy their unique status as human beings. The only reliable and true value is that which is in the individual human being in his characteristic individuality.

It is this characteristic individuality that precludes the possibility of equality of men in the egalitarian sense, and the Conservative recognizes that any attempt to force men into an egalitarian condition can only lead to disaster for all.[37] This could only be achieved through the coercive agency of government that would reduce all to the lowest common level in a general dehumanizing process, where all would be either soulless state employees, workers within the politically managed economy, or pensioners.

The Conservative is not misled into the illusion that the egalitarian process simply requires the taking of property from those of greater wealth and the distribution to those with lesser wealth, in some kind of collective ownership. He knows that a special kind of performance conformity to a predetermined standard is required where each individual talent must be suppressed in order that each does nothing that excels his neighbor. Thus, excellence is excised, and each man is reduced to the lowest common level.

The most productive condition is that in which each individual owns (commands) that property (resources) in such amounts as the fullest expression of his own unique individuality requires. He should not be denied any resources (tools) that he can productively employ in the satisfaction of his own needs and the generation of abundance for all, but neither should he be burdened with property beyond his capacity to employ productively. The Conservative relies upon the institution of the private ownership of property and the competition of the marketplace to achieve this condition with the greatest degree of reliable consistency.

OPPORTUNITY, EDUCATION, AND THE LAW

The subjective condition that the Conservative seeks to conserve is that prevailing social order where each individual retains the maximum liberty to develop according to his own unique capabilities. The foundation of such a social order is the private ownership of property sustained by a system of law. This is predicated upon the knowledge that each individual requires a measure of reliable material security to avoid a dependency status that would work to deprive him of effective direction over his own development.

Given that man requires the ownership of property to enjoy his liberty, that liberty to develop his own unique capabilities is in accord with his natural condition of freedom, and that men are possessed of unequal capacities for competition in the acquisition of property, the question follows: "How can any but a few secure to themselves this natural condition facilitating development?"

The substance of the question carries the answer with undeniable force. Equality of opportunity is the essential companion to the private ownership of property in the latter's role to secure liberty as a condition of man. This signifies no less than the opportunity to acquire property in its fullest sense. All noncompetitive barriers that frustrate the individual in his quest of property tend toward the unnatural limitation of development and are thus non-Conservative in character.

The Conservative carefully avoids actions directed toward the suppression of tension and the enforcement of harmony. Tension is understood as a natural product of competition. Tensions that are generated through Conservative competition are constructive in nature, and through resolution, the development process is facilitated.

Attempts to harmonize society through limitations upon the opportunities of expression will tend toward the frustration of individual and social development. Such limitations will not work toward the transformation of man's inherently dynamic impulses but will deny opportunities of expression through constructive channels of development and thus work to promote expression in destructive convulsions. This is the stuff of which wars and revolutions are made.

"Men do not understand how that which is torn in different directions comes into accord with itself in contrariety, as in the case of the bow and the lyre" (Heraclitus).

Conservative competition is that economic condition of dynamic equipoise characterized by a constantly shifting equilibrium between the requirements of the society and the scarce resources available. The product is *Conservative abundance* defined as that condition of wealth arising out of the unregulated economic activity of individuals and corresponding to their aspirations. This abundance flows out of an atmosphere of competition constantly being resolved in Conservative cooperation.

Conservative abundance has maximum utility when it is reduced to ownership in the individual. Wealth reduced to ownership is property.

Property is defined as interest in its broadest sense. This means any legally enforceable right in the owner to command a resource to his own use to the exclusion of others. In this sense, the concern is with the uninhibited opportunity to acquire a right to resources, the ownership of which will contribute toward the independence of the owner from reliance upon the benevolence or bounty of another for material support in the realization of his condition of liberty.

All noncompetitive techniques employed to sustain an existing property-owner relationship are non-Conservative in character. They tend toward the perpetuation of static relationships and thus frustrate the development that is characteristic of dynamic conservation. The Conservative recognizes that the property owner tends toward the development of a vested interest in the property that his legal rights command. This vested interest will seek expression in a multitude of forms, all seeking to employ some special condition of the owner to reinforce his competitive position.

For example, various types of trust devices are employed by the owners of large concentrations of property to insulate the property from the risks of competition. One of the more extreme examples of such a device is the testamentary trust with the spendthrift provision. This operates to provide the beneficiary with the benefits of property ownership without any of the risks associated with the requirement to productively manage the property. The tendency is toward the perpetuation of a static and thus non-Conservative condition.

There is another characteristic non-Conservative disposition that relates to the employment of the noncompetitive devices and techniques to gain an advantage. This has less to do with the support of an entrenched vested interest than in capitalizing on a particular relationship in order to gain a noncompetitive advantage relative to another who cannot claim the relationship. This involves the destructive techniques of favoritism or prejudicial action in any of its many forms. Wherever an individual is relegated to a noncompetitive disadvantage because of his relationship to a particular race, ethnic group, religion, family, fraternal organization, union, etc., this constitutes the employment of a non-Conservative technique. Wherever an individual is accorded a noncompetitive disadvantage because of a special relationship of similar character, this too is the employment of a non-Conservative technique.

The Conservative rejects the introduction of any noncompetitive devices and techniques as legitimate means of acquiring property. In practical application, this means that any prejudicial treatment on the basis of race or religion is equally destructive and tends to frustrate Conservative development of the individual and, through him, the society. The converse is equally destructive. Thus, the prejudicial treatment of blacks or Jews is non-Conservative in character and must be rejected by the Conservative in entirety. The employment of the non-Conservative device of counteracting force is equally destructive. Thus, where an individual or group seeks to favor an individual by reason or his race or religious relationship to compensate for some prevailing prejudice, this technique too is non-Conservative in character. Prejudice or favoritism is equally non-Conservative and destructive. Not only are such techniques of discrimination clearly unjust, but also their application tends toward the noncompetitive acquisition of property and the consequent frustration of the market mechanism to facilitate the passing of property into the most productive hands.

The Conservative position is identified with the natural condition of individual development and, through it, community development. To frustrate development would be to seek a static society and thus would be an unnatural condition. The Conservative concept of property is not a static or passive one but is dynamic and active. A condition is sought where the maximum of resources available to ownership are continuously exposed to the competitive risks of the market mechanism in order that they constantly pass from the weaker to the stronger hands. It is in this way that the property is most productively employed to generate the maximum available to ownership by all.

Unless there is unrestricted opportunity to prepare, the elimination of the static devices that perpetuate a condition of noncompetitive ownership and the elimination of noncompetitive barriers or bridges to job opportunities would be less than effective in achieving the fluid dynamism required of development. The enjoyment of the opportunity to acquire property bears a direct relationship to the opportunity to make the necessary preparations to compete effectively. The elimination of employment barriers would be barren of Conservative consequence unless they were accompanied by elimination of barriers to the acquisition of education and training.

Two requisite conditions must prevail if there is to be unrestricted opportunity for each individual to acquire the education that his developmental capacities require. The facilities must exist, and then there must be access to those facilities, unlimited by any consideration other than ability to profit from the use.

Before pursuing either of these two points, it should be emphasized that the responsibility for education places all other observations of method and technique in perspective. First, the Conservative looks upon the matter of the child's education as the responsibility of the parent. This parental responsibility is not diffusible and is not transferable to the state.

The Conservative never regards the individual as a resource of the state to be cultivated by the state to achieve some "national goal." Any concept that the state is other than the responsible servant of the individuals who comprise the society is non-Conservative in character. It follows that there can be no "national interest" in education. The matter of education is a matter of local cognizance directly related to the parent, who has the ultimate responsibility.

The family unit existed as such before the state. The family occupies a position in society coextensive and never subordinate to the state. The state has no legitimate role to perform within the family unit except where the administration of the family is such as to deprive one of the individual members of his inalienable rights.

Great importance is attached to this institution of the family. The social unit alone has the capacity to provide the harmonious and secure atmosphere within which the young may develop to maturity, equipped to sustain their self-development as adults. The family is the natural unit within which the sheltered development of the immature individual can be achieved in an organic atmosphere without being subjected to the potential destructive burdens of direct social competition. It is the protection of the infant and the guided development to maturity that infuse the balanced strengths in the adult individual to meet life on its own terms, free from the sheltering arms of a paternalistic social order.

The role of the state, with respect to the family, is to provide that social atmosphere in which the family unit thrives, coextensive with the state. Just as social order is essential to the healthy development of all the members of society, so family order is fundamental to the development of the nonadult individuals within the unit. As social order is predicated upon respect for the legitimate state authority, so is family order founded upon respect for the legitimate state authority and so is family order founded upon respect for parental authority. Under all circumstances, the state must avoid any actions that diminish or otherwise detract from parental authority within the family unit.

These observations have particular significance when considered in connection with the moral and academic education of the children. Where the state has a legitimate role to play in providing the facilities and the personnel to administer the education to the children, the state only arrogates to itself, at the risk of illegitimacy, the authority to determine absolutely the content of that education. The state must remain in direct contact with the parents and must remain supersensitive to the parents' attitudes and desires. All tax-supported educational institutions must scrupulously avoid advancing sectarian concepts and ideas to the nonadult mind. This hazard is particularly present where the subject of "social studies" is presented by teachers who lack the intellectual discipline to avoid the presentation of some political or social bias.

Local control over the education apparatus is essential if the parent is to discharge his primary and ultimate responsibility. This is a fact under circumstances where the parent has very little choice other than to enroll the minor child in a public school. The public school system exists for the single legitimate purpose of facilitating the discharge of the responsibility of the parent to provide for the education of the dependent minor child. The school system emphatically does not exist to provide the mechanism through which the state educates (i.e., trains) individuals according to some standard of adequacy. The parent must always be in a position to exercise effective control over the functioning of the apparatus that exists to assist in the discharge of the parental responsibility.

The Conservative is not insensitive to the requirements of a modern society for a highly sophisticated education product and in no way minimizes the role of the professional educations in the production of the product. It is acknowledged that without his guidance and service, the product could not be realized. The service is indispensable, but service it remains. It is never a legitimate function of the professional educator to attempt to usurp the responsibility of the parent in the education of the dependent children. Wherever there is manifested a tendency to transfer this responsibility to the state, the Conservative must resist on the basis of fundamental principle.

The education apparatus is subject to the same tendencies that characterize all institutions. The managers, here the educators, become increasingly restive under the bothersome relationship of close and effective control exercised by those to whom they are legally responsible. The devices employed by managers to remove or insulate themselves from effective control are many, and as often as not, peculiar to the particular institution. They all have one recognizable common characteristic. They all tend toward the same end: escape from bothersome control.

There is no difficulty in identifying this tendency at work within modern corporate management, where the manager is also a director setting his own compensation, frequently in the form of stock options and other forms of equity ownership. This tendency is clear in labor union management with lifetime chief executive officers, single-party politics, and management use of union funds to advance partisan management advantage. The politician is exposed through his constant efforts to introduce more "democracy" in government. What he wants to do is replace representative control with some nebulous mechanisms of "responsibility to the people."

In the education institution, the propensity is clearly manifested in the university situation where the educator-manager wages his constant battle against the alumni, the state legislatures, and the public. This resistance is frequently accompanied by arguments couched in the language of "academic freedom" (here recognizable as another name for freedom from responsible control). The professional educator-manager goes a step further than some in asserting that he is uniquely equipped through training (discipline) to know what is best and thus should be left free of meddlesome interference by untrained parents, etc.

None should expect the educator-manager to candidly admit that all he really is after is the same free hand to manage that which is characteristically sought by all institution managers. He does, however, come a good deal closer than most to acknowledging the truth of the matter. The arguments are all there. The proclivity should not be all obscure.

When knowledge of this management characteristic is applied to the current arguments concerning American education presented by the politician and his educator-manager handmaiden, the tendency is clearly revealed. The reader should not necessarily conclude that this tendency represents a conscious act of "elite think" on the part of the educator-manager and the politician. This simple fact is that they are what they are, managers, and as such, subject to "management-itis" or the inclination to seek autonomy to utilize the sophisticated skills and talents for which they were employed. The susceptibility is as natural as it is inescapable. The point of the matter is that they are thus unreliable counsel at best when it comes to how the particular institution should operate in the interest of satisfying the needs of the parent in the discharge of his responsibility. Certainly, it is appropriate to take counsel from the politician and education-manager, but such counsel should be conditioned by the knowledge that the counselor has a vested interest in his management position.

So much of the American school system has taken on a non-Conservative character that it is difficult to know where to begin consideration. Some idea of the extent to which the thinking of prominent educators and politicians has departed into the non-Conservative realm may be seen from the very terminology that is employed in discussing the activity. The educator no longer refers to himself or herself as a "teacher." He describes his task as that of educating the youth of the nation. Note, he no longer thinks of his task as that of teaching the pupils entrusted to his care; he has discarded the idea that only the individual can educate himself with the assistance and the guidance of an inspiring teacher, and he now conceives of his role as part of the greater collective role of "educating the youth of the nation."

One of the principal reasons that he has come to think of himself as an "educator" and not as a teacher is because, in many instances, he is intellectually unqualified for the infinitely more demanding role of teaching a precise subject. His training has been in method and technique as a substitute for knowledge. Often he has become no more than an instructor in the particular subject with which he deals. He relies upon psychological gimmicks as a substitute for inspiration and enthusiasm for the knowledge he imparts.

Many of the educators and the politicians have come to think of the youth of the nation in collective terms as some kind of national resource to be cultivated to serve some national purpose. The national bureaucracy has come to rely heavily upon such devices as the withholding income tax, conscription, and regulatory coercion to serve their ends. The politician-bureaucrat has developed such a vested interest in the proceeds of the withholding tax system that he now manifests a definite interest in the productive capacity of the individual to produce the revenue itself. The politician-bureaucrat has come to think of the citizens as a national resource to be exploited for his revenue-producing potential or enforced service. The citizen is presented with the powerful alliance of the politician-bureaucrat who seeks the training of the youth of the nation to serve the purpose of generating tax revenue and conscriptive service or just planned economic growth and the educator who seeks to escape the burden of local control working toward the same goal: national control over the education system.

This tendency to escape local control in the overly ambitious teacher, the restive educator-manager, and the politician must be resisted at every level. Wherever the non-Conservative tendency manifests itself in a reduction of the direct responsiveness of the school to the parent, the Conservative must oppose on the basis of principle, and where the responsiveness has been reduced, the Conservative must actively seek to restore the relationship.

The American citizen is pressured by the ruling elite to accept "Federal Aid to Education." First of all, the title that has been applied to this particular federal activity is misleading. What is in fact proposed is that the federal government be empowered to disburse tax revenues derived from the citizens of the several states to selected public education institutions to supplement the locally generated revenue.

Any way one looks at the pie, this would authorize the federal bureaucracy to decide, for example, that Bridgeport, Connecticut, had an "adequately supported school system" and that Los Angeles did not. The federal government, then, could actually take the property of the citizens of Bridgeport and send it over to Los Angeles to subsidize the school system there. Now the citizens of Bridgeport might be very happy to help out the "underprivileged" fellow citizens in the "city," but might they also wonder just a little bit about the equity of such a system? At best, it may be difficult to convince the citizens of Bridgeport that the people of Los Angeles are not shirking their responsibilities to tax themselves to provide for their own "adequate" schools and thus are shifting their own responsibilities from Los Angeles to Bridgeport through Washington, D.C.

It would seem at least probable that when the next bond issue came up in Bridgeport, some of the more self-interested citizens might suggest that Bridgeport plead poverty like the "Big City Boys" and thus "not adequately" support their school system and thereby qualify from some of that good Dallas money. Once this kind of thing catches on, it is hard to see just where the citizen who finds himself burdened with the support of his own system and that of several other communities won't try to lighten his load in the only way open to him. He will vote no on local bond issues and cut down on his local tax support. Now, where does all that support come from? Right, "federal aid." And who controls the "national school" system? Right again, those who disburse the tax money to pay the bills or, more accurately, the politician-bureaucrat who is hired for this purpose. Where? Right again, Washington, D.C.—out of the biggest department of the federal bureaucracy, the Department of Health, Welfare and Education. At this time, we will likely find the name changed to something more appropriate to its total function, perhaps "Department of Human Resource Development and Maintenance."

On such evidence, a valid prophecy could not be constructed as to the exact course that a policy of federal tax support to local systems might take, but it takes much less imagination to conceive the picture described here than it does to accept the line that no control will follow the "aid" (tax subsidy). No matter how attractively done-up the bait, the risks of getting caught are just too great, and the Conservative must thereby decline to take the line.

The prospects of reduced local financing for the public school system would seem to be more than just a hypothetical supposition. At least, it should be reasonably anticipated that the ratio of local financing to federal financing would steadily shift toward the federal side of the ledger. As this happens, the already strained income tax system will begin to creak and groan even more under the burden. If deficit financing is employed to compensate for the lack of tax revenue, money will become scarcer as inflation costs mount to eat up the buying power of the funds available.

Reference to other federally financed building programs and institutionalized activities is instructive. Is it not the political consideration of where the votes are that determines where the VA hospitals, the army bases, the new post offices, etc., are to be built, expanded, or retained? It takes a great deal of imagination indeed to believe that the money available for the construction of a new school will not be spent where the unemployed building trades craftsmen are able to bring the pressure to bear and not where the school is actually needed. The problem of overcrowded classrooms can be deferred one more year, and the problem of several hundred "hard core" unemployed buildings trade craftsmen with all the voting members of their families is always urgent. The significance is not the plight of the unemployed voters but the fact that the building of schools will be a "public works project" that will tend to put the scarce school dollars into the wrong place, and the consequence will be a general deterioration of the productive facilities.

To be sure, there will be a flurry of activity in the initial phases where some real local deficiencies are relieved by the infusion of federal tax money. This might have the initial effect of allowing some population centers a period of grace before they will finally have to accept the responsibility that is theirs, to provide for the education of their children. This will give a superficial appearance of the program achieving its announced purpose, but just under the surface, the atrophy will commence and the institutionalization of the "national education" system will have begun with the inevitable result of reduced educational opportunities for all.

The Conservative must aggressively oppose any attempt by the federal government to intrude into the locally financed and controlled public education apparatus. The training of children is not the legitimate responsibility of government. It is only the responsibility of government to provide the service of tax-supported education facilities with equal opportunities for all. The public school system must remain most responsive to the persons having the first and final responsibility to provide for the education of the young: the parents.

This is essentially a negative position of resistance to the intrusion of the federal bureaucracy. These negative arguments simply work to preserve the integrity of the system and thus facilitate the maximum responsiveness of the system to the real needs. This does not ensure that the needs will be met. Equality of educational opportunities requires the energetic implementation of positive Conservative principles if all are to share in the abundance and thus live a life of liberty.

Traditionally, the Conservative accepts free public education, available to all who can profit thereby as a fundamental condition of national stability where universal suffrage is identified with citizenship. Not only is the education necessary to the acquisition of property to secure liberty, but also it is necessary to the wise discharge of the duties of citizenship to participate in the government.[38]

The Conservative views the problem of education as a local problem that requires a local solution. If a particular school district in Philadelphia, for example, is not adequately supported and thus equal opportunity is not made available to the inhabitants of the district, it is the responsibility of the Conservatives in Philadelphia to address themselves to the problem locally. It is never enough to simply resist the intrusion of some external authority; it is mandatory that the fertile ground that invited the intrusion be laid waste by the elimination of the deficiency.

If the problem is one of inadequate tax revenues available to support the system, then it is the responsibility of the Conservatives to take the initiative and to tax themselves to generate the revenues required. The salutary effect will be that the deficiency will disappear and the Conservatives will take a greater part in the direction of the local school affairs since it is their property that is burdened with the support of the system. The system will yield a superior product under the influence of Conservative guidance, and the result will be citizens better equipped to compete in the market; thus, an ever-increasing abundance will be generated for all.

At the outset, it should be again emphasized that the Conservative is a realist. He identifies with the course of spontaneous human development. He neither seeks to obstruct the course, nor does he attempt to shape the development according to some premeditated ideal concept of what future society should be. All his energies are devoted toward facilitating the development along Conservative lines, which simply means to maintain a fluid equilibrium so that all future development can proceed along spontaneously constructive lines. From this point of view, the Conservative considers the matter of restricted opportunity through race segregation in general, and public school segregation in particular.

All arguments as to whether continued segregation of the races is socially desirable, whether integration is in the interest of blacks or in the interest of whites, whether the Supreme Court exceeded its authority, or whether the decision calling for the desegregation of the schools with "all deliberate speed" was legally sound have become historical and thus, though edifying, are but academic in interest to the Conservative. The course of natural spontaneous development is clear. The races will live in nonsegregated communities. The forces at work to bring about desegregation are overwhelming to the forces that may seek to perpetuate the conditions of segregation of a bygone era.

It may well be that racial segregation was a natural social condition during one period of the development of the United States, but even if this is so, that period is clearly behind us. The Conservative accepts this as fact and thus seeks not to obstruct desegregation but to influence its course along traditional Conservative lines so that traditional values are not destroyed in the process.

The lesson of the Civil War is clear, where non-Conservative radical elements sought to destroy an entire society in order to overcome the resistance of the non-Conservative reactionary elements who tried to breathe life into a dead institution. The whole of society suffered grievous wounds because the Conservatives were unable to influence the development along natural constructive lines. The Conservative should be fully aware that the efforts of the non-Conservative reactionary to frustrate the efforts of the non-Conservative radical now could lead to a temporary frustration of a constructive development trend that would ultimately overcome the barriers with convulsive and destructive force. It follows that where there exists within the community segregation by race, it is the role of the Conservative to actively seek to facilitate the desegregation process along naturally constructive lines.

The fact of the matter is that continued segregation by race no longer, if it ever did, facilitates the realization of individual liberty to all. The fluid nature of our society has all but eliminated any protection that blacks may have enjoyed from the demands of competition for which they were as yet unprepared. If this argument of paternalistic regard ever had any legitimate force, it has none today.

The action of the Conservative within his community to facilitate the desegregation development should be expected to expose him to the hostility of the radical reformer as well as the reactionary obstructionist. This will be accepted as just another of the risks that must be, as a consequence of being dedicated to the concept of human liberty. We might well take counsel from the American patriot Patrick Henry, who responded to the call by saying, "I know not what course others may take, but as for me, give me liberty or give me death".[39] And remember that so long as one man among them languishes in servitude to that degree, our own and the liberty of all is vulnerable.

Conservative action does not mean that the individual Conservative can take refuge behind the comfortable shelter of Supreme Court decisions, and grand pronouncements of the "law of the land" must be obeyed or rely upon the dispatch of federal troops or United States marshals to enter the community to implement token desegregation "with all deliberate speed." He is acutely aware that the cause of liberty is not yet won and that it will never be secure from non-Conservative assault. Jefferson's words ring clear today as they did when he first uttered them: "The price of liberty is eternal vigilance."

The Conservative is sensitive to man's injustice to man and cannot but view with sympathy those who actively seek economic and social justice for all or any who are oppressed, but he must resist those who would impose a degree of regimentation on society in order to raise the opportunity level of some. He is fully sensitive to the potential tragedy if forceful regimentation were the mechanism through which desegregation was achieved. What bitter fruit the tree would bear if blacks were to achieve parity with his fellow citizens only to find that liberty had been lost in the process!

While continued public segregation of the races is inconsistent with constructive development, the social conditions facilitating desegregation have not developed apace in all communities. The Conservative is compelled to deny his support to those who would forcefully accelerate the process beyond a constructive pace. This means that the Conservative must address his energies to the finding of local solutions to problems of segregation and discrimination that work to deny opportunity to any individual to acquire an education according to his capabilities; a job according to his abilities, skills, and talents; and a property according to his capacity to compete. To facilitate the orderly realization of this condition of nondiscrimination by reason of race, the Conservative seeks the immediate elimination of any barriers to the exercise of the individual's right to vote. This means the elimination of all subterfuge devices designed to achieve the racial discrimination without relying on race identity for application. These devices are easily recognizable as unrealistic poll taxes, literacy tests, resident requirements, etc. This does not, however, mean a support of the intrusion of federal authority into the constitutionally reserved power of the states to set eligibility requirements for the office of voter.

The non-Conservative radical will criticize the Conservative, who now seeks to influence the course of desegregation, for having only chosen to join the forces of desegregation when the battle is about won. The non-Conservative reactionary will point his accusing finger and cite desertion as the principal indictment. The Conservative will realize that each accusation is as inaccurate as it is natural.

The role of the Conservative is to conserve the society, to maintain the equilibrium within which the constructive forces will work toward the continued development of civilization, and to provide the atmosphere within which individuals' liberty will prevail.

The aggressive non-Conservative radical, exuberantly courageous, constitutes a social catalytic agent that sparks the development process. Where the energies of the non-Conservative radical are in accord with the natural and constructive development forces, they will serve to accelerate the change. Vested interest has a role to perform that resists ill-timed and ill-conceived radical reform impulses.

It is the Conservative's role to moderate the process to ensure that the vested interest will not be destructively swept away by unnatural radical trends and to see that forces of reaction do not frustrate constructive development. The Conservative would do well to remember that once the catalytic character of the non-Conservative radical has spent its constructive force, there will remain a troublesome vested interest in the "cause." This must be made to come to terms with the new condition, or be effectively isolated.

There are several facts that the Conservative must keep clearly within his field of vision as he pursues his difficult role in this area of race relations. The condition of race segregation arises out of a background of the institution of slavery. A characteristic of this institution was the commercial character that was unrelated to conquest and war. Blacks were acquired by slave traders in Africa much as one purchases a harvested crop. Those who purchased these human beings acquired property in them as in any other chattel. Prevailing morality required a rationalization. This took the form of the concept of an "inferior race." The corpse of this residual concept hangs today like a stinking albatross about the neck of the nation. The dilemma is ours, and none can virtuously point the accusing finger to another. Pious pronouncements and the striking of moral postures will ill serve the cause of liberty under all circumstances.

The forces of radical change and of reaction are engaged. These forces have become institutionalized to a rather disturbing degree. The institutionalized forces of radical change will characteristically develop a vested interest in the controversy and thus will be compelled to pursue the controversy far beyond constructive limits. The forces of institutionalized reaction will wax stronger and more militant as they become more directly engaged with the forces of radical change. And not the least significant, the power of the federal government will be used to overcome entrenched opposition where this threatens success in an atmosphere where force has replaced the operation of law.

The popularly elected Executive will be unable to resist the pressure for intervention, no matter how restrained his disposition. If the community is left prostrate and bleeding after the controversy has passed, it will be greatly attributable to the failure of the Conservative to effectively play his role in preventing a destructive confrontation between the radical and reactionary forces.

The Declaration of Independence expresses clearly the Conservative concept of the nature of equality of man. "We hold these truths to be self-evident; that all men are created equal; that they are endowed by their Creator with certain inalienable rights; that among these are the rights to life, liberty, and the pursuit of happiness."

Each human being is born free to realize his fullest capacity for development. This is man's natural state, and any external limitations that tend to interfere with the expression of man's unique capacities are frustrating to his natural development. The Conservative believes that each individual is born with certain inalienable rights[40] that legitimate functions of government cannot abridge. Among these rights are the rights to life, liberty, and the pursuit of happiness

To these, the Conservative would add private ownership of property. This is recognized as indispensable to the realization of liberty. Note also that the inalienable right is to the pursuit of and not to happiness itself. No pretense is made at a description of a universal combination of circumstances that will yield individual happiness but rather recognizes that each individual, in the richness of his unique personality, will seek this condition in an infinite variety of ways. The Conservative seeks to conserve the social atmosphere within which each will be at liberty to avail himself of the equal opportunities to pursue this state.

Within a society where the law is the highest authority over the interests of the citizens to realize their rights and where the essence of equality is opportunity, equality before the law is an indispensable condition to the realization of the natural condition of man. This is the very meaning of the symbol of blind justice. Justice[41] is incapable of distinguishing between men and can only decide on the merits of their cause. The Conservative rejects entirely any concept that one individual is entitled to treatment before the law different from that accorded to another.[42]

It is the very recognition of conflicting interests between the individuals of the society, and the society and the individual and the concept of equality that requires and sustains the system of law. If the system of law is to achieve its unique function of avoiding the despotism that is characteristic of systems of "justice" responsive to administrative objectives, etc., equality[43] before the law is an indispensable attribute. This means not only equality between the litigants to a civil dispute but between the state and the accused in a criminal action.

The United States political institutions are the very embodiment of the system of law. They are rooted in the common law and the Constitution, providing for specific remedies for specific complaints. The system flows from precedent through precedent, ever broadening as it responds to the unique features of each succeeding controversy.

The system itself embodies a framework of procedural safeguards that work to provide the equality before the law without which the system would founder on the shoals of inequity. For the system to function at all, it is required that each law must have general application such that each individual citizen will be subject to the same legal application. The Conservative does not recognize any distinction between litigants or those brought before the bar based upon their particular relationships or affiliations.

Perhaps most perplexing of the problems associated with realizing the full measure of equality before the law relates to the very procedural safeguards that work to protect the individual in the exercise of his legal rights. The property at the disposal of the accused has a very real bearing upon whether such accused can make the fullest use of the legal rights available to him. This has to do with every phase of the legal proceedings from the preliminary investigations through the conduct of the trial and, finally, on appeal. It is clear that money is required to defend a criminal action, and only the destitute, the indigent, are eligible for the aid of the state.[44] What is true of the criminal action where the accused is faced with all of the resources available to the state is similarly true where one litigant encounters another of substantially greater resources.

Equality before the law requires that the procedural safeguards be subjected to continuing review that they may be modified to yield an ever-closer approximation of equality. The cost of defense should be reduced wherever possible; heavy penalties should be imposed upon police authorities who suppress evidence favorable to the defense or inconsistent with the state's theory of the defendant's guilt; rules of evidence should be constantly subject to review to facilitate getting at the facts; trial procedures should be simplified so far as is consistent with the conduct of an orderly trial. In civil actions, increasing use should be made of the pretrial techniques of investigation and refinement of the issues, and "trial by ambush" should be relegated to antiquity.[45]

Wherever the Conservative sees crowded dockets with caseloads such that trial of issues are delayed for substantial periods of time, he recognizes a condition where equality before the law is in jeopardy. Where the law becomes the ally of the affluent against the economically weak, the system itself becomes vulnerable. Protracted delay works to the advantage of the party with the greatest economic staying power. The Conservative lends his fullest support to those modernization trends in procedural matters that facilitate the speedy and orderly trial of issues, but this is always conditioned by the fullest appreciation of the value of established procedures in safeguarding the essential rights of the individual. Never could the Conservative cooperate in the sacrifice of one individual safeguard under the cover of expediency, economy, or efficiency.

Where the trial of issues cannot be accelerated through procedural modifications without sacrifice of individual safeguards, the answer is clear. The Conservative will press for an expansion of the judicial system through the constitution of additional trial courts, the appointment of more magistrates, and the increases in judicial budgets.[46] The price of liberty is not only eternal vigilance but also expensive.

There is a modern trend in the administration of the law that is deeply disturbing to the Conservative. This is the tendency to constitute special tribunals, boards, and commissions that have the effect of placing the matter of justice in the hands of administrators. Most frequently, the administrators are not bound by the precedents of the common law or even by their own prior decisions in similar matters. They are not required to conduct the hearing or the trial in open court and, in many instances, are not bound to give reasons for their judgments. Often the administrator or his servant is the judge in his own cause. In many other cases, these decisions are not subject to judicial review. Frequently the hearings are conducted without procedural safeguards, and the burden of proof has been shifted from the state to prove the allegations to the defendant to disprove the state's contentions.

This multiplication of administrative agencies superintending ever-widening areas of the affairs of the citizen is incompatible with liberty and directly contrary to the legitimate functions of government. It is not the function of government to massively intrude into all aspects of the lives, the affairs, and the interests of the individual and to arrogate to itself the role of mediator, referee, conciliator, and judge of all man's business. It is not the legitimate role of the Executive of the government to assume the role of the independent judiciary and to seek to regulate every fact of the lives of the citizens. The Executive must remain subject to the law and never become the law unto itself, for this is the road to the rule of men and despotism. Once the administrator assumes the administration of justice, justice regains its discriminating sight and begins to distinguish between men. The merits of the cause become less significant than the political affiliation, the association, the condition, or the relationships of the litigants. Equality before the law disappears in the selective vision of the administrator.

CONCEPT OF GOVERNMENT

The idea that the government that governs least is the government that governs best has positive meaning to the Conservative. He does not conceive of the act of government as some sort of a crusade to be waged for the purpose of achieving some elusive utopian state but as an art to be practiced to achieve real and practical results. He addresses himself to real problems and actual deficiencies and searches for workable means to treat these conditions. The means selected are never subordinated to the ends to be achieved. The means and the end must always be reconciled one with the other. They must all lie within the legitimate area of government cognizance.

President Lincoln advanced the thesis that it was the appropriate role of the government to undertake those enterprises and engage in those activities that the people either could not do or do so well on their own behalf. When this concept of government's proprietary role is viewed from the perspective of its source, we find a characteristically pragmatic conservative idea. Such a pronouncement is to be understood as coming from one of profound humanity, deep attachment to liberty, the dignity of man, and the dedication to the matters of independence and individuality. In this sense, it is to be understood as relating to the art of government and not to any doctrine or dogma.

The Conservative would understand the government proprietary role thus and would advance the additional observation that it is the responsibility of government to advance the enterprises and the activities to such a stage where they can be managed and administered by the private citizen. The Conservative sees the proprietary role of government as one of constant change and complete absence of legitimate vested interest. It is the role of government to refrain from usurping or preempting any economic area. It is the additional duty of government to divest itself of all proprietary interests wherever possible. This continuing procedure ensures that the unique capacities of government are not dissipated in the management of enterprise that is more suitably owned and managed by private interests. The government thereby remains free to pursue activities in those areas that appropriately fit Mr. Lincoln's definition.

The matter of divestment should be related to capitalization, incorporation, and distribution of equity ownership to private interests. If this divestment were correlated with debt retirement through government bond conversion to equity interest, a useful factor is introduced into the whole area of "big government," finance, debt, and taxation.

Only a dogmatic adherence to some doctrine of political-economics could underlie any idea of "once a proprietary function, always a proprietary function." This and vested interest in an expanding bureaucracy feeds the engine of government expansion. The Conservative can admit of neither and relies on the concept of government as an art to support his concept that all existing proprietary functions are open to continuing review.

The government that attempts too much becomes cumbersome, unwieldy, inflexible, and unable to respond to the ever-shifting requirements of a dynamic society. The Conservative cannot sacrifice the essentially organic and responsive character of legitimate government in favor of some doctrinarian concepts of economic, social, or other types of determination. Preoccupation with theory has a tendency to obscure reality, and the theorist will find it difficult to see the trees for the forest; the art of government becomes lost in the inflexibility of dogmatic approaches to human problems. The individual is lost in the "big picture."

Throughout the full scope of the Conservative attitude toward government runs the idea of limited and limiting government. In effect, the objective is to keep all concentrations of power within manageable limits. The idea is to conserve the environment in which the individual will be best equipped to assert effectively his right to live free. This involves recognition of the fact that where the individual is confronted with powerful social forces unresponsive to his individual interests, this conservative environment is threatened. The individual must rely upon his government, deriving its just powers from his consent, to secure him against power concentrations that would subvert his liberty. This does not mean security from the responsibilities that are naturally his. It is not the security from the risks and hazards of living as a free man that are implicit in the tasteless "welfare state." This means a security to practice his liberties, to realize his inalienable rights, and to achieve the fullest development of his personality, which lies within his unique capabilities.

This does not mean that the Conservative is without long-term objectives and relies upon expediency to prompt his governmental decisions. Quite the reverse is the case. Conservative judgments and actions are grounded on the tested foundation of historical perspective. There are no handy reference works as of the Socialists in *Das Kapital*, and the *Manifesto*. The Conservative's guide is, however, infinitely richer and more reliable. These are the works of the American people, the English-speaking peoples, and the Western civilization.

Principal long-term objectives are contained in the fabric of the nation itself, its antecedents, its origin, its institutions, their structure and fore, the Constitution, and the system of law. The controlling and fundamental long-term objective is to conserve the essential forms of law and government so that a free and orderly society will endure, permitting each individual to realize his liberty such that he will be encouraged to satisfy his aspirations and the needs of those dependent upon him and thereby contribute to the abundant life for all.[47]

It is the legitimate role of government to encourage each individual to be as productive as he is able, for it is in this way that the maximum abundance becomes available to all. The natural means through which this is achieved is through free economic competition. This does not mean the economic anarchy but a system that takes cognizance of the unequal talents, the unequal gifts of men, which accommodates their infinite variety of characteristics and provides for and facilitates their development.

The government's function is to exercise restraint upon the existence and the actions of great concentrations of economic power so that constructive competition is not inhibited through monopolization of the market, the resources, or the site. This does not mean, however, that the monopoly can simply be deprived of its inherent destructive nature through the expedience of government regulation. The efficiency of large scale or the achievement of some social objective is never a convincing argument for the preservation of monopoly, where the consequence is to prevent constructive competition with the accompanying loss of liberty to the individual. Liberty always has its price, and if this price is a less efficient commercial operation or less institutional security, then the price will have to be paid.

Liberty requires that each individual must retain the unrestricted right to prepare for and pursue any occupation that suits his ambitions and his capacities. Each citizen must remain free to formulate and pursue his own economic goals. A general condition of equality of opportunity need prevail, and it is the role of government to influence the society in the realization of this condition. Involved is equality of opportunity under a system of law to prepare, to work, and to acquire property. This requires the general and uniform application of the law and never permits the selective application in order to achieve some social end deemed desirable by the administrator, no matter how popular the objective.

In particular, the Conservative must be sensitive always to the non-Conservative tendency to employ the agencies of the government as a countervailing force to correct an imbalance between two destructive concentrations of institutionalized power. This technique is always attractive to the popularly elected politician who lacks integrity of purpose and seeks simply to moderate the conflicting forces to sustain his own power position.

One particularly unsettling manifestation of this technique is the treatment of labor-management relations. Antitrust laws are employed with punitive effect against business while monopoly practices are encouraged within the oligarchy of coercive labor syndicates. When union management demonstrates characteristic monopoly-institution derelictions, the remedies are to introduce coercive governmental power to "restore a balance." With each such introduction of government authority, essential liberty is abridged. "When the elephants battle, the mice get trampled under feet."

One of the characteristic weaknesses of democracy is to thrust little men into positions of power. The result is to induce a condition where these little men respond to collective pressures in which the rights of individuals are balanced against their political associates and are prejudiced in the process. The form of the Republic is constructed so that the destructive acts of these popular "leaders," who equate personal courage with doing what is popular and politically expedient, will be contained within tolerable limits. The Conservative is keenly aware of the tendency of the ambitious demagogue to arrogate to himself power and remains ever vigilant in defense of the fact and the vigor of the separate institutions of government, with the system of checks that maintains the political power diffusion. This is the essential basis for the Conservative defense of the federal system.

Government's role is to provide an atmosphere of security within which the individual remains free from the interference of others to practice his liberties. The art of government is one of action and restraint. Action in preventing interference by a foreign power, action in eliminating license and privilege, and restraint from interfering with or inhibiting the functioning of all those other social institutions that facilitate the development of man.

VII
ECONOMIC GROWTH, ABUNDANCE, AND THE ESTATE

A Conservative society is more than a society in which the essential material needs of man determine political action. It is a society where the total of the human personality is encouraged to grow and flower in all of its individualistic richness. This requires a rejection of the rather crude and unsophisticated concepts of Marxism with its single materialistic bias. This also requires a rejection as inadequate, those political ideas based upon the rudimentary evolutionary concepts of man's origin. Material well-being, to be sure, is a condition of the Conservative society as is law and individual liberty. But the former must never be confused with the latter. Just as individual liberty cannot long survive without a system of law, it only thrives in an atmosphere of abundance.

American history is filled with accounts of the lives of uncommon men who gained their education, as Lincoln, on the frontier by firelight in the log cabin or who rose from humble beginnings to positions of wealth and power, as Carnegie, or achieved greatness despite disabling physical handicaps, as Edison and Keller. There is much evidence that genius will rise to the top as cream despite all obstacles. It may even be that some greatness is the product of adversity and privation. It is even probable that genius is honed and polished by hardship.

Much as the Conservative values genius with its creative capacities, he remains aware that it is each individual, the common and the uncommon, that is the ultimate human-social value. Genius is just one of the many human attributes that blend together in the uniqueness of the individual human personality. It is the well-being of each working toward the full development of his own unique capacities in an atmosphere of liberty that is the Conservative social value. The Conservative knows that the greatest number of men would be denied the opportunity to develop under conditions of extreme want. Their personalities will wither and perish under the destructive burden of poverty.

The more abundant the society, the fuller will be the development of the personalities of the individuals untouched by genius. The satisfaction of the human appetite works to liberate the individual from the dependency status in which want and privation tend to hold him captive. As a captive of poverty, the development is frustrated. It is not, however, the simple relief from material wants that liberates man. The relief must be accompanied by a right to the relief enforceable against all other individuals and institutions within the framework of the system of law. This means rights of private ownership of property enforceable in a court of law. Nothing less will do.

This decidedly does not mean a right to apply for relief from an administrative agency or to petition for assistance from some state bureau but means to command the resources to his own use not as a matter of privilege but as a matter of right.

As each individual develops and in turn contributes to the general development of his society and his civilization, each individual's capacity to employ more complex and sophisticated devices to facilitate the further development of his capabilities expands accordingly. Advancing technology places more complex devices at the disposal of each and thus tends toward the wider diffusion of the culture to ever-increasing numbers.

For example, in the Washington Territory, little more than one hundred years ago, there could be found copies of Shakespeare, Milton, the Bible, *The Greek Classics*, *The New England Primer*, and Webster's elementary spelling books, all transported west in the cupboard of the Conestoga. This was the culture the technology supported. Now stand great radio and television stations, theaters, libraries, and countless other instruments to bring the full richness of the world's cultures to the very doorstep and living room of the descendants of those intrepid pioneers.

As each is raised, or more accurately, is left free and encouraged to raise himself above the bare subsistence level, he gains time and energy to expend on the development and the refinement of his intellect, his talents, his appreciations, and above all, his morality.

Once an individual's appetite for food is reasonably satisfied, his appetite for books, music, art, drama, and all of the other attributes of the highly developed culture engage his active interest. There appears no predictable limit to man's capacity to employ more and more resources in support of his own personality development. As each attains a higher stage of development, his capacity to employ additional resources productively expands, as does his need and disposition to do so. This escalation and sophistication of need and want for additional goods and services are without practical limit.

Who among us would be so bold as to hazard that at some predicable time all man's wants for music, for arts, and for literature would have been met and that there would be no further need for composers, for painters, and for writers?

It is in the context of this understanding of each man's need for increasing resources to nourish and sustain his own development that the Conservative understands the matter of "economic growth."

The Conservative does not regard "economic growth" as a positive social value unless it contributes to the liberation of each individual to achieve his own maximum development. If the consequence is simply to burden the individual with additional quantities of consumer goods in order to sustain a condition of "full employment" in a kind of planned factory-to-mouth cycle of forced draft economic activity, economic growth may, in fact, be restrictive of liberty and thus undesirable.

Before dismissing the idea that economic growth may be undesirable, consider but one example, the "farm problem." Those who practice the art of "growthmanship" measure the GNP for each succeeding year against the last. If there has been a percentage increase, then they will conclude that there has been economic growth, and if there is a decrease, the conclusion of "negative economic growth" (whatever that is) follows.

There lingers any doubt that surpluses filling government warehouses are counted with the GNP for the year in which they were produced. Where the nation not blessed with a bountiful farm year with the consequence that the nation's farmers lose a substantial portion of their crops, put the case that no more is produced than all of the individual consumers can or are inclined to consume—growthmanship—economics tells us that the nation did not enjoy growth to the extent that the farmers failed to produce the mountains of surpluses of the year before.

The growthmanship economist becomes frightened and is gripped by anxiety. The condition demands the employment of the whole arsenal of political-economic weapons at his disposal. The paradox, incredible as it seems, is to expand the scope of the government intervention that introduced and aggravated the condition in the first place.

The Conservative views this kind of economic growth as something to be avoided as being destructive of liberty. Public ownership of unusable property that burdens the individual with the duty of diverting some of his property to the idle function of maintaining the surplus property deprives property of its productive function in support of the liberty of the owner.

Economic growth generating planned surpluses year after year is not only an illusion but is just plain waste. The farm resources are wasted in surplus production. Persons who would otherwise be productively occupied in some other line of work are induced by the subsidy to stay on the farm. Finally, the property of the individual is taken from him in the form of taxes to support the whole wasteful program and thus is unavailable for real productive use.[48] For there to exist "Conservative abundance," the production of goods and services must be usable by the individual in the support of his liberty. The goods and the services produced must correspond to the real needs and aspirations of the individual members of the society.

The Conservative views the "science" of economics as essentially descriptive in nature and is extremely skeptical of the capacity of economics to reliably project the course of the future. Economics is an immature discipline that engages the interest of many brilliant and some not so brilliant minds.

When economics is elevated to the level of a science having the capacity to predict future political and economic trends, it takes on many of the characteristics of scientific "fortune-telling." When economists are employed by politicians to recommend political policies to achieve a degree of mastery over the undisciplined forces of the society and the marketplace, we are reminded of the "frontier snake-oil salesman" with his "genuine" straight man. It was not many years ago that German bankers employed astrologers to predict the business cycle, and alchemists were the protégés of monarchs who sought to escape the consequences of their own fiscal mismanagement and improvidence through turning base metal into gold.

The time may come when economics will have matured as a science to the point where it can, in fact, do some of the things that the non-Conservative now claims for it, but that time is not now. Certainly, the degree of attention that the subject receives from so many inquiring minds promises great things for the future.

There is an old New England folk saying somewhat as follows: "If you fool me once, that is your fault. If you fool me twice, then that is my fault." Apply this to the concepts of the "mature economy," "underemployment," and "pump-priming" devices to treat economic "recessions." Remember that President Roosevelt described the economy as mature during the Depression years and looked upon the basic problem as one of distribution. It should also be recalled that after all the years of "New Deal" spend for prosperity, the unemployment or "underemployment" figure stood at a staggering ten million. This was 17 percent of the available workforce just prior to mobilization for World War II.

There is no reliable evidence to support the thesis that the New Deal succeeded in bringing the nation out of the Great Depression. There is much to support the opposite conclusion. The diversion of resources from uses that would have followed out of the workings of the marketplace, in fact, prolonged the Depression.

It is not necessary to be suspect of the motives of a past politician to suspect that he was, in fact, wrong. The humanitarian motives of the New Deal need not be disputed. When citizens are without bread, the civilized thing to do is give them bread. This the Conservative will not debate. But to base a whole pseudo-science of political economics on Depression psychology is quite another thing.[49]

We are told we are an "affluent society" by presidential advisor and Harvard professor J. K. Galbraith. We understand this idea the professor is putting across to his readers somewhat as follows: "The Affluent Society" is one in which the economy of that society has "matured" to a point where the substantially unregulated functioning of the market cannot be relied upon to sustain the required economic growth and maintain full employment perpetually. In such a society, it becomes necessary for the government bureaucracy to funnel off the excess capital (uninvested savings) of the people (individual citizens) and put it to work in the "public sector," which seems to be but another phrase for "public works projects."

This is about the way this idea is understood by his non-Conservative adherents as demonstrated by their actions.

The labor-union manager, who feels just a little insecure in a condition of underemployment that threatens his union's institutional monopoly, is encouraged. He need not consider the elimination of nonproductive featherbedding practices because all we have to do is spend in the public sector and full employment will reappear.

The building contractor who finds that he has greatly overextended his production facilities during a period of artificially stimulated home building need not make any painful economic adjustments because all that is required is to spend in the public sector and full employment will return.

The unemployed steelworker who has seen the need for the product of his mill diminish, need not think of another line of work because all that is required is to spend in the public sector and the underemployment will disappear.

The impression that seems to be left in the minds of those who read or hear these ideas falls into two broad classes. The Conservative remains unsure whether the professor is really serious and is antagonized by the presumption on his intelligence through the proffering of the panacea. The non-Conservative seems to be either relieved or elated or both. What seems to lie just beneath the surface is a Conservative belief that the time is well nigh to begin paying for past economic sins and a non-Conservative nonrecognition of sins at all.

This kind of economic thinking is pure sophistry.[50] The proponents are not putting forth serious proposals founded on a solid knowledge base but are putting out just what they think the public will buy. This presumes on a trust that is not just unethical but approaches the immoral. To carefully avoid serious consideration of the impact of fiscal mismanagement following the involvement of the United States in World War I and lasting without interruption to date is to attempt to sweep one troublesome but inescapable fact under the rug.[51]

Much comfort cannot be taken in the fact of the existence of the Federal Reserve System of regional central banks and member banks. Almost since the creation of the Federal Reserve System in 1914, the political expedient of inflation has been pursued as a policy of government. The deflationary collapse 1920–1921 followed the inflation of World War I. This was followed by an "easy money" policy through the 1920s and then the collapse of 1929. The Great Depression stubbornly persisted through the 1930s despite all the spend-for-prosperity efforts of the federal government and the easy-money advocates. In 1940, ten million remained unemployed when another war rescued the advocates of "easy money" and "spend for prosperity."

World War II was financed in the usual politically expedient manner—borrowed money. This would not have been so dangerous, but for the fact that much of the debt was monetized, that is, represented the sale of bonds to commercial banks in amounts in excess of the savings on deposit. The result was to create Treasury accounts against which the government could write checks to pay the costs of waging war without withdrawing any property from the citizens. This is exactly the same, in effect, as the printing of money. Carried far enough, the folk saying of "not worth a Continental" might just be superseded by a more modern version of "not worth a dollar."

Because of the total commitment of the economy to war, the demand for the goods that would otherwise have been purchased with these manufactured dollars in the hands of business and individuals was deferred until after the war. Inflation resumed its destructive course in 1946 with $70 billion of monetized debt in existence. The first effects were apparent in quality deterioration because of the price controls, but as the controls demonstrated their characteristic weaknesses and were removed, the full flight of inflation was resumed in the form of rising prices and declining purchasing power.

Some would be inclined to dismiss the foregoing as just a pessimistic appraisal of the events that flowed out of the easy-money policies pursued without significant interruption since World War I. Some would grant great confidence to the fashionable economic experts of the day. These credulous people might profitably direct their attention to the pronouncements of the fashionable economic experts of another day—that day immediately following the conclusion of World War II. At that time, there was widespread apprehension that the deflation of 1920–1921 would be repeated and fears of a depression of 1946 were widely held and advertised. The federal government was urged to adopt strong measures to cope with the high numbers of anticipated unemployed.

The oracles of economic doom were entirely in error. Had the nation acted upon their counsel and armed the federal government with the additional power thought required, the result would most certainly have been to surrender additional liberty and most probably have made it an irresistible temptation for the politicians and the bureaucrats to exploit the power to cope with the imagined crisis. The economic distortions that would have resulted could have substantially arrested the healthier readjustment with the consequence that the situation that we face today would be even more critical.

Even after being discredited by events, the easy-money advocates have succeeded in addition to the inflationary pressures almost without interruption through 1957, and since then, with each deficit year, the forces are fed. Deflation will follow inflation just as assuredly as night follows the day, and as the engine of inflation was fed by spend-for-prosperity schemes, the deflation will be driven to the depths of depression by those who use the powers of government to distort the economy.

Inflation is disruptive to the development of "Conservative abundance." This is the only kind of economic growth that can be relied upon to nourish and sustain liberty. The effect of inflation is to introduce distortions into the lives of individuals where the otherwise sound basis for economic decision that the free market facilitates is complicated by the speculation of anticipated declining worth of the dollar. Businessmen look for "windfall" or unearned profits in goods where the effective demand far exceeds the supply available. Productive facilities are expanded on the basis of the distorted profit picture. Organized labor tends to demand a share of the windfall profits, and since the profits are to a degree unearned, the management acquiesces easily. The hope is that the windfall will be just enough bigger later on to compensate for the uneconomic settlement.

Business management and labor management develop a vested interest in the continuation of inflation. Owners of shares of common stock benefit as their apparent profits increase as dollar earnings per share respond to the impetus of inflation. As inflation psychology takes hold, the prices of the shares are bid higher and higher as more and more individuals and institutions speculate on continued inflation and attempt to guard against the probability. Real property owners realize substantial unearned profits as more and more easy money chases after the limited land available. The traditional virtues of industry, thrift, and husbandry are replaced by idolization of consumption, speculation, and indolent leisure.

Much of the advantage that accrues to the businessman, the workman, the stockholder, the real-property owner, and the speculator is accounted for through the shift of real wealth from the defenseless, the pensioner, the annuitant, the holder of savings bonds, the owners of money deposits, and from all the rest of the individuals who were just not strong enough or clever enough to get enough of the new "worth-less" dollars for the old "worth-more" dollars to make up the difference.

If the strong were unable to thieve from the weak under the cover of inflation, this method of gaining a noncompetitive advantage over another would lose much of its attraction. There is an old proverb, "Take the profit out of crime and crime will substantially disappear."

The tragic and immoral consequence of inflation, as public policy, becomes apparent when one witnesses the lot of the aged and considers those retired or who have been reduced to a dependency status at an age when he or she is defenseless and thus must rely upon the largess of the benevolent federal government to sustain himself or herself at a subsistence level through Social Security. Their liberty has been stripped from them, and election following election they must slavishly cast their vote for the candidate who promises to increase the size of the Social Security welfare check.

The American people have not yet begun to reap even a small portion of this tragic crop of prodigality we have sown. Frightening is the prospect of the day of reckoning. What a bitter harvest will be reaped by those wage earners who have been seduced, through the easy-money policies and the spend-for-prosperity inflation, to pilfer their insurance and retirement funds by living beyond their productive means.

The temptation will be great to shift the burden of past improvidence to future generations through the same expedient patent remedy that fostered the disease. This is a bit like a drug addict who seeks to avoid the painful withdrawal symptoms through taking of more drugs and who holds out to his child the only remedy he knows to still those accusing eyes. Make the child an addict too. Oh, where is the spirit of the nation that responded to the stirring words of Paine in 1776: "Rather if there be trouble, let it be in my day, that my child may enjoy peace." We have danced to the tune. Let us now resolve to pay the piper. We dare not delay one more day except at the greatest peril.

Persons who have realized personal profit from inflation are not the only ones addicted to the drug. The federal bureaucracy has developed a collective megalomania, generated to a considerable extent by the relative ease with which taxes are withdrawn from the expanded dollar income of the individual who has profited through the inflation. Infected by the ease with which the inflationary media has been fabricated through the monetization of the debt, there has been produced a psychosis syndrome of economic grandeur that is potentially disastrous. In the non-Conservative lexicon, frugality has become a sin; prodigality, a virtue; and budget discipline, something to be disdained by the improvident breed of Keynesians who guide the "New Frontier."

Incredible schemes have been devised to subsidize other regimes governing nations, which have not yet reached that level of economic maturity, take off, sustained economic growth,[52] and affluence as we.

They are as yet unable to monetize their own debt and generate their own inflation to underwrite the projects that their planners have devised. The non-Conservative has imposed the burden upon the individual American to authorize and underwrite these foreign aid schemes under the pain of being unpatriotic to resist. To even question the wisdom of subsidizing the non-Conservative Socialist economy of India exposes one to the charge of being a bad word (*isolationist*, for example).

If we inquire as to the compelling reason why the individual American should subsidize the non-Conservative Communist economy of Yugoslavia, the answer is that Yugoslavia is not within the orbit of Moscow. Carry this argument far enough and Albania becomes eligible for aid, and following just one more repudiation, it will become imperative that we assume the full burden of subsidizing the industrialization of the non-Conservative Communist economy of China to help them become independent of Moscow. Once again, we will be asked to subsidize the economy of the USSR because Khrushchev is a "good Communist" and thus deserves our protection from his more militant critics. The reasons and the reasoning are substantially the same. The only reason why a particular proposal may sound incredible is because we have not yet been asked to do it.

When the improvidence of this appropriation of American property and its export abroad by the spendthrift non-Conservative administrations is reflected in a flight from the dollar by foreign financial interests, the remedy is not to reduce the government export of capital but to impose restrictions on American business operating abroad. The answer to the consequences of the destructive economic practices of the federal government is to restrict the activities of business.

Again, the curious propensity of the bureaucrat is to restrict the generation of "Conservative abundance" in the name of economic growth. Non-Conservative political economics seems to be infected with the Orwellian malady of "doublethink".[53] Scarcity becomes affluence, contraction becomes growth, regulation becomes liberty, words become action, reaction becomes progress, intervention becomes the opposite of isolationism, retreat behind the shelter of the United Nations and other entangling alliances becomes foreign policy, and the security preoccupation of a benevolent despotism becomes the New Frontier. This is the goose-killing paradox.

"Economic Growth," which involves the concept of stagnation implicit, is seeking a four-day workweek, and learning to live with increased numbers of unemployed through a permanent unemployment compensation welfare system is not acceptable to the Conservative. If this is the "affluent society" and the "New Frontier," the Conservative recognizes the basis for his rejection. This is reaction and fear, and the Conservative can have none of it.

The Conservative needs no cleverly contrived catch phrases as the "New Deal," the "Fair Deal," or the "New Frontier" to stimulate him to action. He knows well that there is but one frontier, and this is the edge of the known where man forever stands with his face turned either toward the future with its Sphinx-like inscrutability and promise of high adventure or back toward the known with the illusion of security in material welfare. The Conservative knows that it is not material wealth that will yield him the reliable base from which to drive aggressively into the future. It is the reliable forms of social institutions that provide for a society under a system of law, where man remains at liberty to plan and choose his own goals, where there is equality of opportunity to prepare for, seek out, and achieve the goals that the individual sees for himself where each individual is guaranteed under law the right to the fruits of his labor, where the private ownership of property not only sustains the liberty of the individual but tends toward the accumulation of resources in the hands of those who have demonstrated a capacity to serve the interests of their citizens through the most productive management (productive of Conservative abundance).[54]

Each Conservative knows that a continuation of the present trend toward non-Conservative Socialism will retard the development of the capacity of the individual to be productive. The welfare-state concept,[55] with the characteristic inflation component, can only result in governmental controls over, first, profits, followed by wages, in order of declining popularity. As the controls are instituted, greater and greater economic distortions will appear and economic growth as presently conceived by the non-Conservative political-economic elite will be seen for the illusion that it is, an avenue toward the goal of stagnation first, followed by deep decline.

The inevitable consequence of such policies will be the adoption of an absolute authoritarian regime capable of marshaling the remnants of the once strong free society in the defense of national independence (freedom and liberty will have been lost only to be recovered at terrible cost by our children). This, of course, presumes that the United States will rise to the defense of national independence after all liberty has been lost.

What is to be done? First of all, we must recognize that disaster can overtake us if we persist in living and functioning in a dream world where we believe that we can eat without working; where courage is a thing where individuals seek refuge under the benevolent and welcoming arms of an opulent bureaucracy; where sacrifice means to the other fellow; where our confidence is no longer in ourselves and the institutions that our father sacrificed so much to build, nourish, and defend; and where we stand in fear of our future because we have lost faith in our past. We must restore the nation's faith in the strength and the dynamic force of individual liberty. Confidence must be restored in the essential validity of the institutional forms of our society [56] where the individual is positively influenced to serve the needs of all through the pursuit of his own individual development. We must assert without apology the belief in the validity of "free competition" in the marketplace as the mechanism through which the highest degree of productive cooperation can be realized by free men. (*Free*, of course, does not mean economic anarchy but economic activity subject to law where each is guaranteed the right to the maximum liberty consistent with the realization of liberty to all.)

The destructive burden of inflation needs to be eliminated, for in the absence of this, our strength will be drained as blood from our veins. A great step toward the arresting of inflation will be the substantial reduction in the federal budget, at least to the point where the federal bureaucracy consistently lives within its means.

The largest item in the federal budget is the defense expenditures. This figure alone is enough of a burden on the millions of individual Americans and their enterprise as to inhibit economic development. Without delay, the Defense Department budget should be subjected to the most careful scrutiny with the objective of eliminating all unnecessary items. The fact that each proposed economy will be stubbornly resisted does not excuse any delay in approaching the problem. We must tailor our defense requirements to the long haul and must not permit ourselves to be panicked into costly mobilization and demobilization that characterized the stop-and-go defense policies of the "fair deal" administration. Each succeeding crisis in our international affairs must not be used as an excuse for adding to the already immense burden the nation bears.

Except for those expenditures abroad that are in pursuit of clearly defined national objectives, "foreign aid," or any other federal export of the treasure of the American people must stop. National objectives are defined exclusively in terms of service to the legitimate interests of the millions of individual Americans. Within the terms, the continued export of treasure to subsidize the non-Conservative Communist government of Yugoslavia becomes highly questionable. Doubtful becomes the financing of the grandiose plans of a Nkruman or a Nasser to assist them in harnessing the people of Ghana and Egypt to authoritarian regimes. Precluded becomes the picking up of the check year after year for the non-Conservative Socialist schemes of Nehru, who seeks to avoid the harsh consequences of his bankrupt policies.

Government subsidy programs would be liquidated as soon as practicable. First priority would be given to the costly and pernicious farm subsidy program. The marketing of all agriculture products should be returned to the open free competitive market at the earliest date possible. The plight of many of the farmers is directly attributable to the operation of this subsidy program itself.

Granted, the withdrawal of the subsidies will inevitably work extreme hardships upon some of the farmers least able to absorb and adjust to the changed farm marketing environment. Some limited program of readjustment assistance should be devised on a time and self-liquidating basis to help the less fortunate over the roughest spots, but nothing should stand in the way of discontinuing subsidies as such. This will inevitably lead to the shutting down of some farms and the realignment of others, but the farmer affected will just have to make the adjustment as a responsible citizen in a free society. He must accept that just as no one has a right to direct that he remain on the farm if he chooses another occupation as better suited to his development, so no one has the responsibility to keep him as a dependent subject in an occupation for which he is comparatively unsuited.

Economies in defense spending, drastic reduction in the foreign export of treasure, and elimination of the practice of taking property from one citizen to give to another through subsidies would go a long way toward achieving the required reduction in the federal budget. This would obviate the seeming perpetual necessity to resort to deficit financing and monetization of the resultant debt with the inevitable inflationary consequences.

This, however, will not get the job done until there is a far clearer understanding of what conditions facilitate the thing called "economic growth." More and more equal shares of less and less cannot succeed in the long run, even though some of the currently less affluent may eat better for a few weeks. You just can't slaughter the breed cattle as Castro did in Cuba and expect to have a bumper crop of calves the next year. What must be recognized is that the only meaningful economic growth means millions of individual Americans going to work in occupations of their own choosing, earning and keeping the product of their labor to save or spend as they as individuals see fit and becoming more and more productive as each develops greater skills and gets his hands on more productive tools.

What is required is a disposition to face the facts. Work, thrift, and husbandry are the traditional virtues that are the vital prerequisites to an abundant future. These human virtues are as indispensable today as they were when the Pilgrim Fathers sat down to the first Thanksgiving and looked back in thankfulness for having been granted the grace to survive on the rock-bound New England shores.

There never seems to have been, and there is no evidence now, that there is a simple formula for success. The good life is not a life of ease but a life of liberty in which each man is permitted to assume the risks that are his to claim in the independent development of his own unique capacities. To claim this right, man must first demand that he not become the ward of a solicitous state. Each man must be afforded the opportunity to acquire property to employ in the service of his own personality development. To make this a practical possibility to all, Conservative abundance must be a general social-economic condition.

Business, private business, owned and operated by individual Americans risking, working, and hoping, is the source of Conservative abundance, that abundance which is available to private ownership of individuals in support of their liberty. It is this abundance which is the object of economic growth. This is not the meaningless growth of mountainous farm surpluses. This is not the anachronistic growth implicit in the continued maintenance of old forts, bases, or depots, which have outlasted their usefulness except for the patronage political purposes. This is the development of the business of producing goods and services in response to an existing or anticipated demand. This is useful and useable production, meaningful production. This can be the reorganization of a business that permits it to compete more successfully in a free market despite the fact that the reorganization simply involved the disposal of burdensome properties. This is the growth implicit in cutting out the fat of a business that puts the enterprise in better competitive trim, even though this involves a reduction in the total workforce. This kind of growth comprehends the modernization of a plant facility or the introduction of new machines to put better tools in the hands of the skilled workman.

To achieve the condition of Conservative abundance, the maximum amount of property must remain at the disposal of the individual citizen to be employed as he sees fit. This means that taxation must be reduced to and maintained at the lowest possible level consistent with the actual government's requirements to discharge its legitimate functions. It would do us well to recall the historic American answer to the Barbary pirate's demands for tribute, "Millions for defense. Not one cent for tribute." Tribute is tribute regardless of whether it is paid to a foreign potentate, the bosses of some powerful collective lobby, or the ruling elite of a liberal democracy.

The total tax burden should be reduced as rapidly as possible, and the tax upon business enterprise should be reduced substantially immediately. The burden of a 52 percent take from the profits of all corporate enterprise earnings over $25,000 per annum is an immense depressant upon growth. The degree to which this burdensome tax has already prevented the required modernization of production facilities and damaged competitive capabilities in the export market is beyond calculation.

We are told that we have been pricing ourselves out of the world market, that our labor costs are too high. The non-Conservative then tells us that we must lower tariffs and subsidize our weaker industries to compete. There is even some acknowledgement that some tax concessions should be made to the businesses that wish to modernize. Note well, however, that nowhere does the non-Conservative suggest that business enterprises be liberated from the burdens of excessive taxation in order that each can seek its own solution to the particular competitive problems with which it is confronted.

Be not confused by the specious and seductive argument that this 52-percent tax take comes out of the pocket of some wealthy executive or Wall Street millionaire. One look at the run-down machinery of American mills should be enough to dispel any such illusions. This tax-generated deterioration is nothing more than the technological equivalent to Dr. Castro's slaughter of breed cattle. For a substantial number of years now, some of the wages and the taxes of some American businessmen have been nothing more than the eating up of the tools with which production must continue. The witticism of Lord Keynes that "after all in the long run we will all be dead" becomes a tragic travesty on the condition of those who have outlived the consequences of their own improvidence. Just sixteen years after the collapse of Nazi Germany and the liberation of Europe, we are told by the non-Conservative political-economists that we "have no alternative" but to join or come to terms with the powerful European Economic Community. But to do this, we are asked to subsidize more noncompetitive industry. Once more, we are urged to take the product of the labor of our productive citizens to distribute to the less productive. This we are urged to do by the "popular leader" in the "national interest."

The Conservative answer to those who now wail again at the wall is "Take the monkey off their backs." Turn the American people loose. Free the millions of productive individuals from the bondage of the welfare state and let them compete. With the banner of freedom held high in the hands of 186 million plus individual Americans, competing as free people, all external challenges will be met. Let America export its heritage and birthright instead of the sterile material technology unaccompanied by the condition of individual liberty. If man gains the world, he gains nothing if he fails to gain his liberty in the process.

VIII

UNDEREMPLOYMENT AND THE STATE

Because of the broader connotation, the term *underemployment* is used instead of the more common but far more limited term *unemployment*. Underemployment implies idle resources of all types as well as unemployed individual workers and those employed at levels below their full capacity to produce. The term is taken from the concepts of economics arising out of the Keynesian "General Theory".[57] It has particular significance to those who have rationalized criticism of the policies of the "New Deal–Fair Deal" through a calculated projection of the "General Theory." It is reflected in a doctrinaire faith in the capacity of government to constructively intervene in the workings of the free economy through monetary and fiscal devices to control or at least substantially influence quantitative economic activity.

$Y = C + I$ and spend for prosperity—this is the formula. At the bottom of this whole concept is the Keynesian idea that $Y = C + I$ [employment and income (Y) are determined by the propensity or disposition to consume (C) plus investment (I)]. Keynes went on to equate I (investment) with S (savings) on the theory that savings and investment tend to become one.

From these ideas, it is not difficult to see how one can arrive at the conclusion that it is possible to "spend for prosperity." Any time there is less than the maximum amount of Y, all that is required is to add some I. If the millions of free citizens don't have enough I at the time (note that I is the same as S), then the government just stuffs some bonds (S or I) and pumps this I into the economic veins of the nation, and automatically

Y increases and "underemployment" disappears. Y is maximized, and we have a condition of "full employment".[58]

The Employment Act of 1946 is a reflection of the thinking of the "easy money"[59] and "spend for prosperity" proponents, but perhaps more than this, it is a direct reflection of the labor union management's desire to escape "paying the piper" for the unearned increment exacted from a people whose attention was diverted by crises and war. Under the continuing threat to withdraw support to the nation, labor union managers[60] have exacted concessions from an acquiescent government by policy and law that compelled many individuals to pay tribute to these managers for the privilege to work.

Operating under a cost-plus defense contract system, businessmen were encouraged to grant increasing economic concessions that had little relationship to the productivity of labor. The concessions were directly related to the critical nature of the work to the defense interest. Recently, we have witnessed a repetition of this same type of regard for the defense of the national interest at the various defense missile projects. At a time when the non-Conservatives were crying "missile gap," the labor managers in their ranks were extorting exorbitant sums for labor under threat of work stoppage.

The significance of the Employment Act was not fully apparent during the immediate postwar years as the nation experienced a period of chronic full employment. This was much to the astonishment of many of the economic doom forecasters who had urged this law. The significance is that under the doctrine that underemployment arises from a shortage of I (investment or savings), spend-for-prosperity becomes the legitimate remedial device, and where there is insufficient I, there will most frequently be insufficient R (tax revenue). It follows that the deficiency must be made upon from DF (deficit financing), which because of the I deficiency, must be monetized with the consequence that I once again becomes I (inflation), and the theory is validated even though by the wish-think process.

In the days of the frontier America, this technique would have been termed rather quaintly as "robbing from Peter to pay Paul," but as frontiers change, thus do dogma, doctrine, and morality, it would seem, for today, this is called "boldness to move America ahead."

Nowhere in the alphabet symbolism is there found Q (quality), P (productivity), W (wage), or PC (production cost). The convenience of this approach to economic problems is that underemployment, depressed areas, or just plain unemployment becomes a fiscal and therefore a national problem, and the individual who might otherwise have to make a rather painful adjustment from his preferential, privileged, or sheltered position is able to shift his burden to others through the federal government with the consequence that "Let the other guy do it" becomes "Make all of the nameless and relatively defenseless individual other guys do it because it is their duty."

The result is to gain a little time at the cost of introducing yet another distortion into the economy that will ultimately be corrected with greater cost to all. For those who go to their graves in advance of the day of reckoning, it may appear that the forest will remain forever so long as the wind agitates the leaves. The Conservative knows that the forest will endure as a dynamic growing thing capable of sheltering man for countless generations, where each generation in its turn lavishes upon the trees attention and care and never demands more of the forest than the forest is at any time capable of giving. The parasites are constantly eliminated; the dying trees are allowed to pass so that the young and healthy growth will be fully nourished and the sucker growth is always separated from the saplings. Perhaps the most important of all, the natural watershed is allowed to remain undisturbed so that the rains are not unnaturally directed into destructive channels of erosion-baring roots and toppling trees, flowing off without performing their natural function facilitating the balanced constructive growth.

Useful as the aggregate concepts of full employment and underemployment are to the social scientist in the study of social phenomena, the Conservative must reject them as keys to political action. The Conservative cannot rely upon statistical rates of growth, production, employment, unemployment, national income, etc., as some kind of automatic triggering device setting off a predetermined amount of government intervention into the free market or inducing a certain annual rate of inflation.

Some non-Conservative political economists actually view a minimum percentage rate of annual inflation as healthy and as a prerequisite to growth. Consider for a moment the integrity of a government that uses a patriotic appeal to an industrial worker to "invest" (loan) in a "share" of America through the payroll purchase of U.S. Savings Bonds, with the prospect that he will have the principal plus interest as a retirement nest egg and, at the time, of the sale, this same government is calculating a systematic theft of the value of his money at a predetermined rate of 3 to 5 percent for each year he keeps the bonds. Many non-Conservatives may look upon this as a clever financing device and technique, but this is just the same kind of cleverness that we witness in the charming, personable, embezzler who sweet talks little old ladies out of their life savings. The fact of the crime is not changed that the little old ladies are so enamored by the smooth-talking fraud that they refuse to admit they have been taken or, if they suspect this is so, just think the price was worth the ride and won't testify. In the absolute, the embezzler is a crook no matter how many times he gets away with the fraud.

When the Conservative sees idle productive capacity, unemployed individuals, scarcity of investment capital, and reduced business activity, he is greatly concerned because he knows that individuals are not in command of the abundance necessary to sustain their liberty. He accepts his individual responsibility for any general economic condition that has grown out of distortions flowing out of failures to maintain the "free market".[61]

He accepts that he, as well as the non-Conservative, must share, as individuals, the consequences of having allowed monopoly, license, and privilege to distort the economic activity of the millions of individuals who constitute the society. The Conservative thus accepts his full share of the responsibility to sustain the unfortunate unemployed individual in his time of need. The obligation is accepted, arising from his role as a citizen. A right in the unemployed individual to this assistance is acknowledged. This is a right that may be asserted with dignity and integrity. It is the right of one who has been victimized through a planned inflation; a conspiracy to invest labor union managers with authoritarian powers and protect their vested power interest through the support of a monopoly condition; burdensome and nonproductive subsidies; a proliferate export of treasure to foreign governments in pursuit of incredible socialistic schemes; and all the other improvident activities of his fellow citizens through the agencies of their government.

It is not enough acknowledging a right to unemployment compensation for a period of time during a time of need. No Conservative can be satisfied until the individual who finds himself without productive work to perform is again productively employed. This can never mean learning to live with a relatively high rate of unemployment so long as the unemployment compensation is high enough as the author of *The Affluent Society* suggests. What is demanded is a condition where all those who wish may pursue occupations of their own choosing and succeed or fail on their own merit. To arbitrarily assign a percentage of the national population to nonproductive idleness is a non-Conservative idea of philosophical bankruptcy.

The starting point of the Conservative concern is the individual who is underemployed (here, we mean a state of employment below that of his optimum productive level, taking into consideration the individual's capacities for work and his disposition and readiness to employ those capacities productively). It is the individual who is underemployed, and the problem is to restore him to a fully productive state. The individual who is underemployed must be provided with the kind of social environment wherein he is at liberty to seek out opportunities to employ his capacities productively and must have unrestricted access to the opportunities that he finds.

Curiously, equal opportunity means a lot of rather special things to a lot of non-Conservatives.

It may mean a condition of no discrimination on account of the color of one's skin but absolute self-assertion of job monopoly on the basis of seniority. It may mean a condition of nondiscrimination on the basis of religious heritage, but a privileged status because the person asserting this idea happened to be affiliated with a particular institution. It may mean a condition of nondiscrimination because of a person's particular ancestry but, at the same time, an organized distribution of employment within the government on the basis of political association.

This non-Conservative concept of equal opportunity, which calls for complete economic opportunity *except* for seniority rights, which must not be disturbed, for a system of favoritism based on religious persuasion or fraternal affiliation or the idea that all is all right as long as it does not affect our patronage, is nothing more than "equality except." This is just the kind of doublethink that so often characterizes the non-Conservative. Here, equality of opportunity becomes monopoly, a license, and a privilege, and the assertion of the individual right to choose is enslavement.

One of the first and more fruitful Conservative approaches to the problem of underemployment could be the elimination of this unequal equality, thereby permitting the undistorted selection mechanism of the competitive market to put the tools of production into the most productive hands.

The political economist has coined another word for us to describe a certain type of underemployment. This is the term hard-core unemployed, the unemployed who has remained in the nonproductive state of a substantial period of time. This particular individual (the non-Conservative would use an aggregate term), has become the subject of much grand pontificating by the non-Conservative Liberal politician. Many now express surprise, bewilderment, and other uncomprehending attitudes that in recent years each time we have experienced an adjustment in business activity followed by a "recovery," this number of underemployed or the hard core of the unemployed has not declined as business has picked up.

The remedies proposed to meet this now "national problem" are many, costly, and varied, but they all have that one recurring non-Conservative characteristic: "Let the millions of faceless, inarticulate, and defenseless productive citizens assume the burden of the wards of the federal bureaucracy." We are told that the Unemployed Compensation System must be standardized (nationalized), that the number of months for which the benefits are to paid must be increased, that the benefits must be increased in all states through federal subsidy, and that a guaranteed annual wage is required (Guaranteed with what? one might ask. Perhaps inflationary IOUs against goods not produced and business not done), as well as profit sharing, relocation allowances, retraining allowances, prohibitions against American business investment in foreign lands, discriminatory tax treatment against some foreign business in favor of another, reduction of tariffs accompanied by additional subsidies (that's right, more subsidies, fantastic as this sounds), and of course, the shot in the arm of more I (inflation) through DF (deficit financing).

In the process, we are told by the courageous talk of the non-Conservative that all this will call for sacrifice. It is not difficult to see what we are being called upon to sacrifice. It is our very birthright of liberty that is to be sacrificed to the non-Conservative Liberal's insatiable appetite for power over all facets of our lives. As power and more power is concentrated in the central bureaucracy under the impulse of benevolent solicitude, the certain issue will be totalitarian democracy.

Now, if all of this was just another placebo to make the patient think good thoughts and to restore confidence in an essentially healthy condition so that he will get up off his pallet and walk, then the matter would not be viewed with such intense concern by the Conservative. This is not a sugar pill, however. It is hooch to the alcoholic. We are on the stuff, make no mistake about that, and each time we get withdrawal symptoms, we reach for another bottle. The snakes and the crawling things disappear into the wall, and we once again look on the world through the pleasant, drowsy haze of a drunk. Nothing bothers us, and we certainly can't see the condition of our liver. What difference does it make as long as we die happy, which has become synonymous in the non-Conservative Liberal mind with ever-increasing consumption, and if we can't consume it, then store it. The mountain of unrefined alcohol rotting in rented grain silos is even rationalized to become a "national asset" instead of a scandal of squandered resources.

The non-Conservative Liberal, whose policies are at the bottom of this whole mess, frequently strikes the dignified pose of the inept pugilist who is being outpointed in every round and addresses his Conservative critics with the plaintive pleas for "constructive criticism." What he really is saying is that the witch doctor with the most powerful medicine is in his corner so nothing that we can say can be more right than what he is already doing. Despite this closed-mind condition, which is characteristic of the doctrinaire and dogmatic non-Conservative Liberal, the Conservative continues to express his opposition and to offer alternatives.

What are the alternatives to treating the condition of "underemployment" as a national institutionalized problem requiring national institutionalized remedies? The first task is one of identifying the problem. The way to do this most certainly is not to generalize from some unreliable statistical index and prescribe general remedies for an imaginary illness. This requires extensive diagnosis, and this means that we must consider the facts and not some doubtful approximation of what we think the facts to be. One of the most fruitful first steps would be to get rid of all the politico-economic faddists and cultists with their doctrinaire and dogmatic approaches to economics, with their bag of fiscal and monetary tricks, and to employ some honest-to-goodness bankers, businessmen, and social scientists to formulate and consider the questions. The true scientist pursues the truth uncommitted to the advancement of a doctrine, dogma, or parochial point of view.

The scientific method that is the most sophisticated tool of investigation available to us and employed by truly inquiring minds could prove of immense value. One of the characteristics of the scientific method in the hands of the professional is the open-end system that never rests on the comfortable supposition that all has been discovered or learned. Here is the essential characteristic of Conservative development to so conserve that the constructive development process is facilitated. The very essence of conservation is the facilitation of the developmental process. There is but one criterion that would underlie Conservative inquiry. No solutions are acceptable to problems that have the tendency to shut the door on further inquiry or which put the individual in jail with the manager, his jailer.

When these problems of underemployment are approached from the scientific point of view, nothing is foreclosed for dogmatic or doctrinaire reasons. This means that deficit financing by the federal government will be considered for what it is and will be subjected to scientific appraisal as to its efficacy in treating a particular problem or family of problems. This same open consideration would apply to such devices as unemployment compensation, aid to "depressed areas," retraining allowances, relocation assistance, and so on. In addition, of course, searching consideration would be addressed to such things as monopoly privilege (business and labor), rigidity in wage structures, economic subsidies, right-to-work laws, closed unions, closed shops, taxation (discrimination and rates), depreciation allowances and plant maintenance, government operations, federal government budgeting, etc. Under the impact of true scientific inquiry, there would be no "sacred cows."

Such scientific inquiry may be expected to point up some promising approaches to the matter of underemployment, which are presently considered outside the dogmatically proscribed area of non-Conservative consideration. For example, it might develop that the rigidity introduced into production costs of a particular business as a consequence of inflexible wage rates is a significant factor in creating idle capacity. It may be that under some conditions, a particular labor monopoly has been able to exploit a monopoly situation to impose a labor price that is noncompetitive and unrelated to the productivity of the labor performed. It is just possible that wage rates that exceed the productivity of the labor performed are reflected in production costs that have resulted in pricing the article produced out of the market. If these are the reasons that less of the particular product is produced and thus fewer workmen are required in the particular business, it would seem just a little difficult to reason that more unemployment compensation can have a result other than to put more underemployed on the "welfare state" dole.

Labor productivity is employed by the non-Conservative Liberal to justify wage increases without limitation to any of those whom they lump together under the collective term *labor*. A classic example if this reasoning process was presented by secretary of labor, Arthur J. Goldberg, addressing the AF of L/CIO labor manager's meeting on December 8, 1961, when he took it upon himself to clarify the remarks made by President Kennedy the day before to the same audience. Here, *clarify* seemed to mean take the sting out of the president's words and remind these powerful labor union managers that when the president said "sacrifice," he did not mean them but really had in mind the traditional sacrificial lamb of the non-Conservative Liberal, those same poor, overtaxed, overcharged, unorganized, faceless citizens.

President Kennedy, to be sure, did not point any finger in the direction of these powerful men, but he did make a reference to "responsibility" in negotiations, and for men like these, just the suggestion of "responsibility" was enough to unsettle a few lunches in the Florida sun in December. The secretary came right back the next day with the reassuring message. He assured these managers that there was "plenty of room" for wage increases under the administration's economic policy. The secretary went on to say, "Inequities do exist. There is no question about it." Note, there was no definition or example of *inequity* given; thus, the president of the United Automobile Workers was free to conclude that his auto workers were paid inequitably and that the President was certainly not directing his remarks at Mr. Reuther, who after all, has always negotiated "responsibly."

Mr. Goldberg went on to state that "we do not propose to restrict in any way the ability of collective bargaining to remove and solve inequities. That is the day-to-day business of trade unionism and we encourage and support it." Note here the use of the phrase "restrict in any way the ability." The secretary is a respected member of the bar who is accustomed to choosing his words with care. Logic compels that we conclude he intended to convey that this administration approved of the monopoly privilege exercised by these union managers and was assuring them that this administration could be counted on to support their privileged status.

The secretary then went on to observe that the president, in taking the sting out of his use of the term *responsibility*, recognized the "necessity to correct inequities" (no definitions or examples yet), "recognizing variations by industry, and by companies within an industry (that) wage increases overall—if we are to keep the economy going on a sound, non-inflationary basis—should be earned by increasing productivity." The secretary then observed with some emphasis that "there is plenty of room for advance in this highly productive country under that general concept of wages."

If this had not been so carefully reported in the New York Times, December 9, 1961, we might wonder if we had heard this articulate labor lawyer correctly, but that is what he said. The secretary first takes note that there are differences between industries and businesses but then moves to a consideration of "overall" wage increases and refers to "increasing productivity." One is forced to take the secretary at his word and conclude that he intended just what he said. Anyone can justify a wage increase under this "general concept of wages," which lies within their own particular productivity or where they are suffering an "inequity" or where there is increasing overall productivity, and then all of the guesswork is taken out of this with the assurance that the "room for advance" already exists.

The secretary then was asked for some instances where a wage settlement had been inflationary or what indices he would use in deciding that a settlement was high or low. He dismissed the question by saying that he "could not answer in generalities."

If there was any doubt left that the secretary was employing the fraternal method of telling the union managers that they had the green light and that the president's use of the term *responsibility* was just a word for other ears, note the remark: "The important thing is whether the overall settlements do not exceed productivity. We are not a monolithic country and ought not to be." I don't intend to begin here a club of "Goldberg-ologists," but I would hazard that hidden within this suspiciously out-of-place reference to "monolithic" is the key to the whole thing, and all good union managers will recognize this to mean that they need fear no action by this secretary that might affect their privileged position.

The secretary went on to make reference to "substandard" wages and to observe that "we are living in an economy which is a divided economy, an economy which is part high wage and part low wage, and in that sector of the low wage economy we can help restore the buying power that exists in the American public and contribute to the general welfare and the business welfare as well." Here, even the "circle-think" treatment of "productivity" is not enough. The secretary talks of an undefined "low-wage economy" with the clear implication that any raise above this undefined level would be beneficial to the "general welfare" regardless of "productivity" considerations. If one has any remaining doubt as to the calculation of the secretary's remarks, the careful distinction between "general welfare" and "business welfare" should dispel them all.

There remains no excuse for those who would take refuge behind the supposition that the secretary did not mean what he said. This man must be considered for what he is. He is a highly successful labor lawyer, ex-general counsel for the United Steelworkers of America, a man who is experienced in the subject to which he was addressing his remarks, and is in the habit of choosing his words with care. It is obvious from these remarks that the secretary does not think of "business welfare" as falling within his concept of the "general welfare," which it is his Constitutional duty to promote. By making this significant differentiation, the secretary is then able, without violating his oath of office, to pursue a policy that is biased in favor of the union managers and hostile to "business." If what he does contributes to the "business welfare" as well, then this will be incidental to the purpose and a "windfall" to business to which they are not, in fact, entitled by definition.

This careful distinction satisfied the ethical requirements of the secretary and permits him to adopt the full-circle type of reasoning with respect to productivity. The purist might wish to know why the secretary so carefully avoided any precision in his definitions, but to the non-Conservative, this is a superfluous speculation, for under the "full-circle" technique, definitions are unnecessary. If we accept the premise that there is "plenty of room for advance in this highly productive country" and that "wage increases overall . . . should be earned by increasing productivity" and this is just another way of saying that "overall settlements do not exceed productivity" and that we accept the additional "inequities" concept coupled with the division of the economy into "high" and "low" sectors, then there is no need to define "productivity" because no discipline measure is involved and we have come full circle, where to assert is to prove.

Wages remain what they are, compensation for the work performed plus any increment attributable to privileged monopoly status (note this is just the other side of the underprivileged status of a nonmonopoly state). There is not even a suggested implication that some wage rates might now exceed the productivity of the worker being paid and that this particular workman enjoys this unearned wage increment as a result of his monopoly privileged position.

This avoids entirely any consideration of the possibility that a "big union" worker being compensated at a rate, for example, in excess of $4.00 per hour, might just be gathering to himself an unearned increment at the expense of one of those "nameless unorganized Georges or Georgettes." The "big union" worker can justify any wage increase that he can exact through the collective employment of his immense monopoly power to not just restrain but to paralyze trade on the basis that his wage increase lies within the "overall settlement" limit. The individual whose wages have not kept pace with the "inflation" (who, in fact, has had some of his property taken from him by the privileged worker) can justify his increase on the basis of inequity, and the union manager who finds that his wage schedule is substantially below that of, for example, the United Auto Workers or the United Steelworkers of America can look upon his efforts as a contribution to the "general welfare and business welfare as well." With this many green lights, who needs a definition for productivity?

This discussion of the words of the secretary of labor addressed to the managers of the most powerful labor unions in the country could be dismissed as just another partisan attack against Mr. Goldberg, except for the fact that Mr. Goldberg has chosen to allege a "general concept of wages" that involves the correction of "inequities" and that "wage increases overall *should* (note *should* and not *must*) be earned by increasing productivity" but that "substandard" wages can be raised in any event regardless of productivity on the theory that this will "help restore the buying power that exists in the American public." This "general concept of wages" should be studied by the Conservative in detail with the object of discovering whether there is any basis for the claim that this will promote the "general welfare and business welfare as well" or whether this is just another evidence of the non-Conservative Liberal tendency to cater to monopoly, license, and privilege within vote-heavy collective groupings. The right question to ask here is whether this "general concept of wages" will tend to diminish underemployment or to aggravate an already critical situation.

It should be abundantly clear that any attempt to measure wages and wage increases according to productivity requires careful definitions. Failure to employ precise definitions exposes the user as being politically and doctrinarian motivated.

Secretary Goldberg has taken a series of personal actions calculated to confound potential critics. He would have us believe that protestations of virtuous intent, divestment of pecuniary interest, and assertions of disassociation from his former employers (the United Steelworkers of America and the AF of L/CIO) have yielded a detachment that now validates his socialistic bias.

There is no need to impugn the integrity of the secretary to question the motives underlying the Kennedy administration's general concept of wages. The basic premise upon which it is constructed is Keynesian and Fabian Socialist in character, and productivity is employed as a subterfuge to obscure the real drive toward economic collectivization and centralization of power. If the labor secretary is not of a socialistic persuasion, he has evidently lent his considerable persuasive talents to those of this Kennedy administration who are.

The tragedy of such a government policy lies in the fact that the condition that it purports to cure is only aggravated. Ever since 1932 and the New Deal, when Keynesian economic theory and Fabian Socialist ideas have substantially influenced the conduct of American government, chronic unemployment has prevailed. Only during war periods and the immediate aftermath has this been interrupted. When this is contrasted with the dynamic performance of the European and Japanese economies as they moved away from socialism, the significance is clear.

Pursuit of this general concept of wages and other such policies will not correct but will aggravate an already deteriorating condition. Only a movement away from government interference in the economy can restore the essential vigor of economic activity that will yield employment opportunity for all, and it is not regimented "full employment" but full employment opportunity for all, which is the Conservative objective.

When business begins to fall off under nonproductive burdens of punitive taxes and artificial wage costs as some potential buyers decide the price of the product is higher than they are prepared to pay, managers are compelled to corrective action. They can attempt to cut costs and reduce the price to induce the reluctant but potential buyer back into the market. They can just cut the price and perhaps sell at a loss for a period of time and hope that general business will pick up and the buyer be induced to pay the higher price later on. They may just cut back on production and wait for the market to turn up again. In practice, of course, a combination of these and other techniques are employed, but rarely will a downturn in business not be reflected in a drive to cut costs.

Under a system of inflexible labor contracts where wages do not respond to changing business conditions, the most attractive way open to management to achieve a reduction in their largest budget item, wages, is to do the same job with fewer people. This is precisely where the management directs its most searching inquiry—into production costs. Any student of the subject knows well how successful the managements of the steel and aluminum plants were in this practice following the decline in metal business beginning in 1958–1959.

In a very real sense, the productivity of the men who are fortunate enough to be still at the machines has increased. Through layoffs, fewer people today are producing a greater tonnage. Now, if this increase in the productivity of the remaining workers is absorbed by wage increases according to the administration's "general concept of wages," no price reduction would be possible as a result of the reduction in production cost; thus, the composite position of the product would remain unimproved and the layoff would be denied its healthful effect of allowing for a price policy to stimulate business. The growing number of "hard core" underemployed individuals who hold seniority rights under Steelworker's contracts is not so mute testimony to the effect of just this "general concept of wages" in application.

As wages are made more and more inflexible, that is, unresponsive to the level of effective demand for the products that are produced by the labor, the inevitable result is to do more and more work with less people. Those persons who enjoy a noncompetitive advantage over their fellow citizens will benefit at the expense of the less favored, the less privileged, and the ones unprotected by institutionalized monopoly.

There is a limited recognition on the part of President Kennedy and his administration that in some instances, American labor has succeeded in pricing itself out of the world market and that it is so weakened by its opulent state that it cannot compete with foreign products without a tariff or subsidy. What we see here is a recognition that in some American industry, individual labor productivity has reached such a low state that other citizens must subsidize these low-productivity high-wage workers in order that similar foreign manufactured products to the ones produced by these workers can be imported on a tariff-free basis. It seems just a little odd that the secretary of labor can talk about "inequities" and the solving of them when he is proposing that the organized machinist who cannot compete with the German machinist, for example, should be subsidized by the soda fountain attendant, the elevator operator, the fry cook, the home laundry owner, and all of the fifteen million plus stockholders in American business. Already this organized machinist has succeeded through monopoly privilege and inflation, shifting the burden of his low productivity onto the backs of the life insurance owner, the pensioner, and other nonprivileged Americans on fixed or inflexible incomes.

The institutionalized efforts to administer wages through various devices as the minimum wage, a "general wage concept" that contemplates the administering out of existence of inequities, the division of the economy intellectually into high and low sectors, and the effort to raise the "low sector" all tend toward a more and more rigid, inflexible wage structure that can only lead to one end: more and more "underemployed." The underemployed will be among the least skilled, the youngest, and the least experienced, the least senior, the least affluent, and all in all, the least capable of doing anything about their condition.

If the author of *The Affluent Society* is correct, all we have to do is learn to live with this increasing number of "underemployed" idle people as long as the "unemployment compensation" is high enough and everything will keep right on cooking along. The unacceptable consequence of this rationalization is the relegation of large numbers of the population to a condition of idleness. A look at history will convince even the strongest skeptic of how dangerous to an ordered society is a large, idle, unpropertied population, which is most frequently concentrated in the larger urban centers. The story has been repeated without significant variation from Caesar's Rome, where the "populares" shouted for bread and circuses; Paris, the barricades of 1889 and the guillotine; Moscow and Leningrad, with "all power to the soviets"; Descamisodos; and Juan and Eva Peron. Now we witness Dr. Castro decrying the need for elections because he rules in the name of "the people."

For those who take comfort in the "inherent stability of the American citizen" and say it can't happen here, the UAW in Detroit and the waterfront of San Francisco in 1934 should be striking reminders of our vulnerability. The Conservative must recognize an extreme and potential danger in this trend toward increasing numbers of citizens relegated to a life of idleness. This is particularly an urban problem. The Conservative recognizes that the problem is not responding to the dogmatic and doctrinaire approaches of the non-Conservative Liberal whose machine dominates most of the largest urban centers. An alternative solution consistent with Conservative principles is urgent if the trend toward totalitarian democracy is to be arrested. When the non-Conservative Liberal's answer to underemployment is placed alongside of the Conservative position, the distinction between the planned and the regulated and the function of a "free competitive market" is cast in relief.

In the current jargon of the marketplace, the Conservative thesis has been derisively termed the "trickle-down theory." In the same vein, it is appropriate to describe the non-Conservative Liberal doctrine as the "pump-up theory." The analogy could be pursued on the basis of the picture of a small stream starting at the top of a mountain, fed by melting snows. As the stream works its way past gigantic obstacles of glacial rocks and through the high Alpine meadows, it remains small, but as it begins to cascade down the hillsides through great green forests and rushes forth into the green valley below, it is joined by countless other little streams and becomes a powerful life-giving river that nourishes the countryside.

Alongside the concept of "pump up," which is synonymous with inflate, there seems little to choose. The consequence of inflation is ultimate explosive destruction of the fabric that contained the inflationary medium. It is true that the illusion of expansion will persist as long as the fabric retains its natural elasticity and can accommodate the infusion of additional inflationary medium, but the point will be reached where the elasticity will become exhausted and inflexibility will take its place. When this transpires, a static condition is presented and then just one more pump and—bang—the balloon goes bust.

The inference is clear. Keynesian political-economic theory is incompatible with the Conservative position. The Conservative understands that the representation of Keynesian theory as a modern validation of the theories of Adam Smith to be a subterfuge to mask the implicit hostility to private enterprise capitalism. The general theory is recognized by Fabian and Marxist Socialists and communists alike as a useful device to obscure the drive toward state-regulated economic activity and ultimate totalitarian democracy.

Those American political economists who have embraced the Keynesian theories have done so less from persuasion of the essential validity of the theories than by reason of their socialistic and totalitarian democratic bias. Galbraith, Samuelson, and Schlesinger are representative of the socialistic totalitarian democrats who have masqueraded under the banner of Keynesian political economics. These men and others of similar persuasion, commanding positions of immense influence in the economics departments of Harvard University, MIT, and other universities affiliated with the Americans for Democratic Action and the League of Industrial Democracy have constantly sought to confuse the student and the public as to the real basis of Keynesian theory. The argument is presented that "laissez-faire capitalism is discredited by history, and that Keynes has come forth as the savior of capitalism." The Conservative recognizes the basic duplicity in this argument where a Fabian socialist is heralded as the savior of the very system he is dedicated to destroy. This is like setting out the wolf to guard the sheep.

The ideas of Keynes are a repudiation of those advanced by Adam Smith in his *Wealth of Nations*. They do not represent a validation of the concepts first advanced by Smith as our non-Conservative opposition would have us accept. The ideas of Keynes are entirely inconsistent with private ownership of property, individually directed economic activity, competition, and the marketplace. When the ideas of Keynes are subjected to objective analysis, they can be seen for what they are and recognized as incompatible with the basis of the Conservative position—liberty.

The ideas of Keynes are not, however, inconsistent with the basic economic theory that underlies the Communist state. These same ideas formed the basis of the economics of Fascism in Italy, Nazi National Socialism under Hitler, and the economics of Argentina under Peron. When the relationship of the ideas embraced by American Keynesians, Fabian Socialists, and international Communists is recognized, the disturbing course of United States policy since the earliest days of the New Deal is no longer so difficult to comprehend.

The decided antibusiness bias of the Kennedy administration could have been anticipated by all those with a disposition to see. This was apparent from the picture of the group of Keynesian political economists with which he chose to surround himself. In 1961–1962, the political-economic "Brain Trust" of the New Frontier was dominated by such dedicated proponents of socialism and totalitarian democracy as Arthur Schlesinger, Jr., Theodore C. Sorenson, David E. Bell, and W. W. Heller.

For those citizens who remained dedicated to the principles of liberty sustained by spontaneous incentive economics and private ownership of property, the dangers were as great as the days when Harry Dexter White and Lauchlin Currie held positions of substantial influence within the economic machinery of the federal government. There is no need to despair. There is a Conservative answer. The Conservative would take steps to restore the characteristic flexibility of the free competitive market.

First of all, this means the elimination of the privilege of monopoly status wherever it exists. Individual security within the industrial society must be found in some other way than in the device of sheltering the individual from the risks of legitimate constructive competition. To achieve an institutionalized security from the uncertainties of free competition, the security of one can only be achieved at the expense of another. This means a policy of privilege accompanied by discrimination, license accompanied by prohibition, and monopoly accompanied by subordination.

Consider how much more socially acceptable would be a policy of wages based upon a flexible formula responding to shifting business conditions, where wages paid to each person adjusted naturally rather than some being forced into a condition of underemployment while others remain at their machines and receive the next regular increase under "the wage agreement," plus an upward adjustment as inflation raises the "cost of living index."

The specific nature of the arrangement should be expected to vary somewhat according to the unique features of each industry and business, but a formula most certainly could be devised, which would not work to deny the employee any of his rights to income but would facilitate competitive pricing and thus active and meaningful competition.

Wages could be set at a minimum figure and a maximum figure. As long as the profits of the business were maintained at a predetermined level, the current or prevailing wage payment would be at the maximum figure. At such time as the profits declined for a predetermined period below a specified level, the prevailing wage payment would be adjusted downward to permit cost reduction to facilitate competitive pricing. The business management could be restricted in the use of improved work methods and technological advances to support workforce reduction at any time the management elected to avail itself of the reduction of wage rate. For each hour worked at the reduced rate, the employee could receive a credit for unpaid wages that would be recoverable out of future profits. For example, if profits recovered within one year, the full amount of the deferred wage payment would be recoverable, and if the profits were not recovered for, say, eighteen months, 75 percent would be recoverable with the percentage scaled down over a period of months. All of this could be related to adjusted management salaries, actual production, and maintenance costs, deferred dividends to stockholders, etc. Each participant in the enterprise would be able to share in the full economic rewards of the business, and all would recognize a continuing interest in its continuing economic health.

The foregoing is not presented as an ideal proposed solution but simply as an example of the type of thinking a Conservative might apply to the solution of the perplexing and seemingly unyielding problem of the chronic underemployment.

One additional observation might be made before we leave this particular subject. This has to do with the government-protected monopoly status of the unions themselves. The existence of this protected status has had a tendency of shielding the management of the large trade and industrial unions from the facts of life, so to speak. What has, in fact, happened is that the management of these frequently monolithic institutions has begun to display the same weakness that afflicts all managements not exposed to the constant selection device of open competition. They tend toward preoccupation with the political problems of sustaining their position. A correspondingly reduced portion of attention and energy is directed toward the prosecution of the real interests of those assertedly served. The tendency is toward a managerial oligarchy with the inevitable hardening of the institutional arteries.

As the individual becomes a supporter or dissenter, as the local union becomes a unit of influence and power, and as regions become areas of political influence, the specific problems of the individual become lost in the need for an industry-wide, regional, or national pattern. There is a tendency to make settlements of real or alleged issues in the interest of sustaining the power position rather than in the legitimate interests of the particular workers involved.

The withdrawal of the privileged status these custodians of monopoly economic power hold would have the salutary effect of exposing the managers to the selection mechanism of competition. The consequence should be a substantial increase of tension as young, militant leaders seek favor among the represented workers. This would be directed toward the pursuit of the substantial interest of the individuals represented and thus would be constructive tension in the Conservative sense.[62]

In this matter of recognizing, through the agency of government, the destructive monopoly character of large, powerful labor combinations or syndicates, care must be exercised lest the real benefits of recognizing the liberty of individuals to bargain collectively be undermined in the process. Since the Conservative rejects the concept of countervailing force as a social stabilizing mechanism, the employment of antimonopoly and anticombination devices against labor monopolies must not be of this character. The remedy must not be simply to "restore a balance" between assertedly opposing forces. Great apprehension arises where the governing bureaucracy intervenes as the custodian and the guardian of the "public interest" to redress the balance between two or more conflicting nongovernment interests.

All antitrust laws and labor management relations legislation embody this countervailing or third force concept. The genesis of this concept lies within the Rousseau-Saint Just-Robespierre ideas of the "general will" or *volonte une*. These ideas are the source of all totalitarian democracy in the Western nineteenth and twentieth century traditions. It is from this doctrinaire source that the American non-Conservative Liberal derives his justification for massive intervention by the government as the "countervailing force."

The Conservative does not subscribe to the concept that there is a natural or historical class antagonism existing between the employees of an enterprise and the owners any more than he accepts the class-antagonism interpretation of historical development of the Marxist Socialist. The Conservative looks upon the essential interests of all individuals associated with a particular enterprise as consistent, one with the other. This interest is to so conduct the enterprise that the economic health will be sustained and the business will be characterized by dynamic growth to the essential benefit of all those associated with it.

The conduct of all associated with the enterprise should be free to respond to the impulse of free economic competition that becomes perfect Conservative cooperation. The tensions that inevitably do arise within this type of atmosphere are resolved and adjusted within the natural competitive context and are not permitted to escalate into great issues to serve the interests of a power elite.

The antimonopoly devices must be sufficiently sophisticated that they will be able to differentiate between legitimate transcending issues and those that are essentially local or individual in character. The use of monopoly power to influence the resolution of essentially local and individual matters should be firmly proscribed. Bargaining for wages should be limited to definable organic economic units and should not be permitted on a geographic or jurisdictional basis. The organic economic units should be defined with attention to the common and related interests of the individuals constituting the units, with emphasis upon the competitive requirements of the businesses and enterprises with which they are associated. The objective would be to sustain individual liberty and to provide the individual with the economic climate within which he can compete from a balanced but unprivileged status within a competitive market.

Within the foregoing frame of reference, the essentially individual and local economic phenomena of unemployment can be seen for what it is, an individual condition of underemployment associated with the broader economic condition of underemployment of resources. From this vantage of organic Conservative perspective, the otherwise institutionalized problem only yielding (perhaps more accurately, unyielding) to dogmatic and doctrinaire treatment becomes recognizable as another system of dislocation within an identifiable organic economic unit. Considered thus, the problem promises response to individual or local treatment, tailored to the specifics of the underlying causes.

If some individuals are unemployed because the stream, which powered the mill wheel, has dried up and the cost of alternative power to run the mill is prohibitive of effective competition, the answer is not the institutional answer of classifying the area on a statistical basis as a depressed area and sending in aid in the form of welfare checks or to capitalize on an opportunity to get rid of some of the building farm surpluses with a "food coupon" subsidy.

The answer is to get the otherwise productive individuals back to work. This involves the sometimes hard choice of withholding any assistance at all, so the people will be forced to face up to the fact that there never will again be water in the stream and that they should seriously consider moving to another locality where the opportunities are more promising.

This, of course, never means the harsh denial of subsistence assistance to tide someone over a tough spot. In the American tradition, this is always the neighborly thing to do.

If a locality has succeeded in pricing itself out of the competitive market such that there is a declining market for the articles that are produced, the adjustment of the price is at least an indicated solution, and subsidies and protective devices, to shield the individuals from the facts of economic life, are just a disservice to them and tend to perpetuate underemployment by making it appear tolerable.

When the problem of underemployment is stripped of its vestments of license, privilege, monopoly, and institutionalized dogmatism, it can be expected to respond to the specific Conservative treatment and substantially disappear.

IX
INDIVIDUAL MOBILITY: SELF-RELIANCE AND DEPENDENCE

The late Charles E. Wilson, when he was secretary of defense, made a remark that has often been quoted and frequently misquoted. The remark was made in connection with a discussion of the then-prevailing condition of underemployment. Mr. Wilson observed that his preference had always been in favor of the "bird dog" as distinguished from the "kennel dog."

Some of the non-Conservative Liberals feigned a rather maudlin attitude of sentimentality and attempted to discredit the secretary by suggesting that he had referred to the "poor unemployed as dogs." Of course, this was nonsense, but it did have the effect of diverting attention from the truth contained in the observation. What Mr. Wilson was saying, in his rather colorful way, was that some people learn early the responsibilities of free men and some lead sheltered lives throughout their days. Mr. Wilson was expressing his preference for self-reliance instead of dependence upon the bounty of another. Specifically, he was suggesting that the person who finds himself in a condition of underemployment should take it upon himself to seek out opportunities to employ his skills and should not rely upon the workings of the institutionalized system to find the opportunity for him.

That this idea should have raised such a furor of irrational reaction from the non-Conservative Liberal is entirely consistent with the Liberal dogma and vested interests. Absence of social flexibility and static relationships among people is fundamental to the Liberal's institutionalized approach to society. Individual mobility is anathema to the non-Conservative position. Class consciousness is to be created and exploited. Conflicts of interest are to be induced and then intensified. Non-Conservative associations are grounded upon these artificial relationships, and all devices are employed to tie the individual to the association in a dependent status.

The non-Conservative cannot rely upon voluntary association. Fact compels a recognition that the interests of the individual and those of the institution are not at all times consistent but, in fact, tend toward conflict. To maintain the institutional strength, resort is had to all types of coercive devices, and in the terminology of the non-Conservative, compulsion becomes free association and the right to work becomes "slavery."

The Liberal doctrinaire never thinks of compulsory association as coercion. Enforced union membership is not intended to interfere with liberty. On the contrary, government-compelled association is calculated to secure liberty and thus cannot abridge it. Within this reasoning context, the non-Conservative Liberal, as all totalitarian democrats, concludes that all who oppose must be perverse, selfish, or subversive. All those Conservatives who resist this compulsion as an abridgement of liberty are identified as being at war with the scheme or pattern of liberty toward which the non-Conservative strives.

Labor unions are institutions within the American society that characteristically exemplify the non-Conservative use of coercion to influence the association of individuals and the calculated development of a dependent status to perpetuate the relationship. It was entirely in character for Mr. Reuther to react so vigorously and irrationally to Mr. Wilson's remark, for the very ideas of individual liberty, freedom to disassociate, and self-reliance struck right at the heart of Mr. Reuther's vested interest as a chief in the power elite or oligarchy of the UAW, and the AF of L/CIO. If such ideas were to gain wide acceptance, Mr. Reuther's hold on the thousands of members of his union could be substantially loosened.

It is one thing to extol the virtues of individual independence and self-reliance, and it is quite another to contrive the environment within which all individuals may be encouraged to enjoy this condition. Just as each person does not possess the same combination of talents and skills, as people are unequal economic competitors, so they have varying capacities for independence and self-reliance. Self-reliance appears to be the product of full development of the individual's personality up to the time that he must cope with a given situation. Individuals seem to possess this quality to varying degrees at different times under different conditions. The individual, completely at home in the city, may become bewildered when in the country. An industrial worker may find himself completely frustrated when he attempts to grow vegetables in the garden. One person may feel a sensation of liberation and exhilaration when he goes on his annual vacation, and another may become so dependent upon his work that he keeps calling upon the office to see how things are going in his absence.

Some individuals are so intimidated by the very fact of living that they are incapable of exploiting a condition of independence to develop their personality. The burden of liberty with its individual responsibility weighs so heavily upon them that they are ground down into a state of depression and impotence. These individuals require some kind of association or relationship to a stable institution to satisfy their need for security. They are, in effect, incapable of finding a sense of security entirely within themselves.

The Conservative appreciates that there is no liberty without security, but he knows that security is not the same as liberty, nor is it a substitute for liberty. The person who experiences the greatest exhilaration of individual liberty with its immense creative force is the person who finds all his requirements of security satisfied out of his own resources even to the point where he has achieved a maximum independence from reliance upon property. The Conservative society accommodates all individuals without discrimination in the favor of one against another. Those rare individuals who have the gift to sustain themselves in the fullest condition of self-reliance will not be driven arbitrarily from the sheltering arms of institutional associations where they have found strength and refuge.

Basic is the recognition that all institutions are but devices, social mechanisms to facilitate the fullest development of the individual. The institution is always recognized as a potential source of strength in dependency and an inhibiting obstacle to the realization of liberty in self-reliance.

One of the essential attributes of the Conservative society is the prevailing condition of voluntary association and the absence of compulsory relationships. The individual remains free to become associated with a particular institution or organization on the basis of his self-interest, as he sees it. He is not to be coerced by the state no matter how benevolent the intent, for this is the road to servitude just as sure as though men were once again sold to the highest bidder on the auctioneer's block. What meaning has the idea of "equality of opportunity" when individuals are coerced or seduced by a benevolent but despotic state from availing themselves of the opportunities that exist?

Anything that inhibits individual mobility and tends toward the perpetuation of static, nondynamic relationships tends toward the denial of access to opportunity just as effectively as though the individuals affected were restricted by race or religion. Equality of opportunity is not a relative term; it is an absolute condition of life to free men.

When considering the matter of individual mobility, one matter in particular takes precedence over all the rest. This is the manner of how one holds his property interests. As we have observed previously, the wealthy are generally in a position to enjoy a greater amount of liberty than are the poor. The rationale is that one who owns or commands enough resources in his own right to assert his independence is thereby made less dependent upon another for his subsistence, and the converse holds true where one must rely on another for the necessities to sustain himself and those dependent upon him. This general observation, of course, exempts those who are either burdened by property ownership or the free soul who can never be enslaved even in prison.

It is the manner in which one holds his property interests that is of significance. This is not to say that the interests are not in themselves important, but it is intended to draw attention to the fact that there seems a vastly greater coercive element present where the interest exists, but the enjoyment is dependent upon a persisting relationship in the holder to another than where the interest is simply not present at all.

When considering the matter of "equality of opportunity," we observed that to sustain his liberty, it is necessary for each individual to have access to educational opportunity from which he can profit in developing his skills to compete and that after he has acquired the skills, he must realize equal unrestricted access to economic opportunity to employ those skills to gain the product of his labor and thereby acquire property. If all of this is to be anything more than a one-shop proposition for each person, where once he makes his choice he is stuck with it for the rest of his life, he must acquire command over the fruits of his labor in such a way that his mobility remains unimpaired.

There are several conditions persisting within American society that tend to impair this mobility and deserve consideration. First, and perhaps the most significant for those affected, is the matter of deferred compensation in connection with employment. This is of particular importance when related to interests acquired under the nature of the interest acquired under Social Security. Of less long-run significance but of greater immediate concern to the affected individual is the matter in which "unemployment compensation" interests are acquired, as well as the nature of the benefits and the related issues of outmoded skills and area restrictions.

Consider first this matter of rights acquired under a system of deferred compensation that are characterized customarily as "fringe benefits" plus any additional property rights that accrue to the employee as a result of his labor but are not remitted to him on a fixed periodic basis. Above all, in restrictive significance are seniority relationships. This particular aspect will be deferred for the present while actual example items of deferred compensation are considered.

Retirement funds are of the first order. The prospect of forfeiting rights to retirement benefits through severance is a great factor inhibiting mobility. With each working year, the dollar value of the right of retirement tends to increase; thus, the potential economic loss increases accordingly. Added to this are the normal "group life insurance" and other insurance benefits plus the not yet general but impressive "supplemental employment benefits."

The Conservative position would accord full support to the conversion of all "fringe benefits" arising out of deferred compensation, or perhaps even more accurately, "retained wages," into mature vested property rights.

This approach should be expected to draw the opposition of both the managers of the business that employs the individual and the managers of the union that represents him. These deferred compensation devices are useful to both sets of managers in restricting the mobility of the individuals affected. For the business manager, these hold the employee to his job, and for the union manager keep him as a member of the union.

The question of practicality has some significance but does not seem to present serious obstacles that could not be overcome through minor adjustments and innovations. The retirement benefits could be converted into a vested interest in the balance of the individual's retirement account. This interest likely would present the fewest problems since most retirement plans are either operated in the form of a trust to which a contribution is made for each dollar earned or an annuity purchased on an established premium basis. The mechanism would simply operate to give the employee a paid-up interest in the trust or a paid-up annuity value as of the date of severance. The consequence would be to facilitate the lifetime accumulation of retirement income regardless of the number of sources, and essential mobility would remain unimpaired.

Insurance, such as life, accident, and health, and hospitalization plans could operate on an extra premium basis to cover the premium payment period of the severed employee for a specified time after severance. Coverage could be limited to enforced severance not for cause and thereby permit the employee to take reasonable time in seeking other suitable employment, without feeling compelled to take the first job that comes along simply to meet the premium payments for his family's protection.

The supplemental unemployment benefit could then be accompanied by a severance payment feature which could only be realized through the forfeiture of all accumulated seniority rights. Consider now the matter of surplus skills and area restrictions. Surplus skills are those skills that have become unnecessary to a particular shop, business, industry, region, or nation, either in the available quantities or in total. The matter of area restriction or geographic immobility is pertinent to any consideration of the matter of surplus skills since two of the more promising approaches in dealing with a problem of surplus skill are relocation where the skill is in demand or retraining to acquire another set of skills.

Many studies have been made, and volumes have been published describing the problem of "automation." The inference is that automation is a new phenomenon that is tending toward the elimination of the requirement for many skills. Automation, in the most general usage, describes certain production techniques where numbers of machines are so related within the production process that they function on command. In effect, this eliminates requirements for operators and helper personnel at the particular machines so directed. Under this type of operation, the machine attendants are more generally maintenance technicians and not operators in the usual sense.

The word "automation" is of twentieth century origin, having been coined or used at about the same time by a director of the Ford Motor Company, Mr. D. S. Harder, and by John Diebold, then a young graduate of the Harvard Business School.[63] The application was not so new, having been introduced into the French textile industry at the beginning of the nineteenth century. What is, of course, even older than the application of automatic machine operation in the production process is the obsolescence of productive skills.[64]

With the invention of the printing press, scriveners became surplus to a considerable degree. The employment opportunities for skilled bow makers substantially declined with the introduction of gunpowder. There is little evidence of any responsible person at the time suggesting the bow maker's or scrivener's neighbors subsidize him in nonproductive idleness.

Technological progress obsoletes jobs. It has ever been thus. The point least understood is that technological progress can only obsolete old skills by first creating the demand for new ones. Jobs or whole industries are only outmoded by advance, which first creates new ones.

The individual who encounters this condition of progress, obsolescence, is faced with the corollary problems of recognition, readjustment, retraining, and relocation.

If there is a community interest in the four Rs of automation or obsolescence, it would appear to rest on a substantially different basis from the idea that where a person is without work in his particular line, he has a right to expect his neighbor, the community, to subsidize him. This means, at the outset, rejection, as discriminatory, any restriction of retraining benefits to a select group of individuals who have found their skills surplus by reasons of automation or technological progress. Equal access to the opportunities of training in new skills must be made available to all, limited only by the capacity of the individual to profit from the training.

Capacity would mean not just capabilities promising of successful completion of the course of instruction but circumstances such that the skills once acquired can reasonably be expected to be employed.

Anticipated skill use requires that the individual be free from any persisting employment relationship that would discourage the use of the newly acquired skills. Thus, an employee on layoff from an industrial plant where he holds recall rights under a labor contract would be required to certify that he had severed all connections with his former employer that might result in his seniority recall and consequently prevent the use of the new skills. This would be one of the minimum obligations of the individual who applied for a retraining subsidy.

Retraining opportunities would be sharply restricted to skills that are not effectively monopolized by any organized group or where access is not open to all skill-qualified applicants. This consideration would have special applicability to trades and crafts of the traditional variety or where any institutional monopoly blankets job opportunities.

This whole problem of obsolescent skills and job loss through the continuing technological progress is but another in a long line of problems of an unregulated and unregimented society seeking to provide each with equal unrestricted access to opportunity. The tools and the techniques that traditionally have been employed to assist the individual to adapt himself to his environment are not unsuited to the current problem. True enough, some more sophisticated devices are not available, but the manner of employment and the social values that guide the use are traditional and reliable.

The American people have always considered the education of the citizen as a common responsibility. This fundamental idea is given form in the great breadth of our tax-supported public education systems and the scope of the private endowment to the nonpublic schools. The use of these education and training facilities has never been restricted to the education and training of the young. Extensive adult education has been a characteristic of the system. The content of the systems have not been academically limited. Early the American people recognized and accepted the requirement for vocational and technical training as inherent within the industrial society.

The non-Conservative would have us believe that a "whole new approach" is required to deal with this problem of the "technologically unemployed." A crisis atmosphere is imagined on the false premise that job and skill obsolescence is a cumulative thing.

Substantially, we are told that it is essential that we authorized the expenditure of federal tax revenue under a federally sponsored program to provide for the retraining of those who have lost their jobs through automation. It is not hard to see that the particular definition that a federal bureaucracy assigns to the words *retraining, automation,* and *technologically unemployed* will have a controlling influence on just who will be selected from among the many individuals who happen to be underemployed to be the recipient of this federal subsidy. Again, we would be burdened with another of those programs to take care of those groups with which the non-Conservative Liberal is forever concerned.

The American people have tangibly demonstrated a general and real awareness of the individual economic problem involved in the loss of a job. The systems of unemployment compensation operative in each of the several states are the expression of this awareness and concern. These systems are of inestimable value in relieving the immediate distress associated with job loss and, at the same time, operate to facilitate the orderly search for new employment. On the whole, these systems work well and are definitely not in the need of some federal program to correct any deficiencies.

In each of the several states, there currently exist technical and vocational training facilities well suited to the retraining of adult citizens. Wherever a local need exists to provide adult citizens with technical or vocational training, these existing facilities are the ones that logically should be employed. The combined use of the existing unemployment compensation apparatus and the existing facilities for technical and vocational training should prove adequate to accomplish the job of providing an opportunity to acquire new skills by an unemployed individual.

When an individual finds himself unemployed with limited prospects of finding new employment utilizing his existing skills, he could apply to the local state department that handles matters pertaining to employment opportunities.[65] This department can be relied upon to have current information concerning local, regional, national, and international demands for skills. In effect, it will have the most current information available with respect to obsolescent and short-supply skills. If the individual applicant's last job was in a surplus skill category, the opportunity could be presented to enroll in a "short-supply skill" course at the local technical training center. Should the individual wish and is otherwise qualified, he could be permitted to enroll, withdraw from the labor market for the time of the training, and draw his regular unemployment compensation check for the period. All of this would be, of course, conditional upon regular attendance and successful progress.

The foregoing system might work rather well in dealing with the mechanics of providing retraining opportunities for those who are qualified. It could fall far short of being any solution to the problem of "technological unemployment," obsolescence, and short-supply skills.

So long as the individual remains tied to his former employment through a system of seniority rights, union affiliations, and retained earnings interests, what reasonable expectation is there that the new skills will be put to productive use? The same critical question applies to those skills that fall under the influence of some institutionalized jurisdiction that limits access to the jobs requiring the short-supply skills.

To ensure that such retraining subsidies are not just another diversion away from the fact that much of the underemployment is substantially attributable to restrictive and destructive practices of union monopoly, much of the obstructive brickwork will have to be dismantled. Care would have to be taken to ensure that the individual retrained is in a position to profit from the acquisition of new skills. He would have to be entirely free from the compelling influences of contingent retained earnings interests with his former employer and would have forfeited all seniority interests related to his former employment. The individual who presents himself for such a retaining subsidy, at a bare minimum, must be qualified and in a position to profit from the new skills. Identification of short-supply skills must be made with equal care, lest obstacles to access be overlooked, which would work to nullify the training. Never must the primary responsibility be allowed to shift from the individual to the state. In the first instance, the responsibility to deal with all the vicissitudes of life lies with the individual. Only where self-help cannot be effective does society have a role to play. This is the Conservative understanding of the Christian principle that we are our "brother's keeper."

Self-help would be infinitely preferable to any tax-supported program. "Self-help" is the enrollment in night or home study courses to acquire the new skills. This involves the individual's own initiative and thus promises the greatest possibility of successful completion.

For self-help to succeed, a recognition is required by the employer of the continuing interest he has in the development of the new skills. An adjustment in work schedules to accommodate training is a minimum requirement.

Some of the largest obstacles to self-help are frequently associated with the inflexibility of union policy respecting work schedules and seniority practices. The problem of providing favorable work scheduling or relaxing of seniority rules to facilitate the retraining of an ambitious employee seem almost insurmountable to much of union leadership.

One preliminary requirement for individual access to retraining opportunity should be the condition that any bargaining unit association that persists must be with a union that does not discourage self-help through work scheduling and seniority restrictions. The minimum should be that the union permits convenient individual work scheduling for ambitious employees, and skills acquired receive preferred consideration for job advancement under modified seniority rules.

What then of the individual who finds himself unemployed in Frontier City, Kansas, and has an employment opportunity in Mid City, Nebraska? Does the community have an interest in assisting this individual to relocate from his present home to the place of employment promise?

It would seem that the community does have such an interest. This is the same interest that is related to the justification for unemployment compensation and compensated retraining. This is the interest in maintaining the essentially Conservative community atmosphere, which is conducive to the orderly seeking after and seizing of opportunity. Relocation subsidies should be payable out of the same funds that underwrite the disbursements of unemployment compensation and related retraining allowances. No relocation allowance should be payable on speculation, and none should be paid except on some reciprocal assumption of appropriate responsibility by the receiving community.

Consider now the case for Social Security. As a point of departure, the Conservative would observe the following points: Private ownership of property is valued for its utilitarian purpose of sustaining individual liberty. The individual is freed thereby from a dependent status for his subsistence requirements. Property ownership has to do with many more things than the accumulation of real estate and consumer goods. In a highly developed industrial and financial society as ours, property is acquired in many forms. Property is money in the form of cash, demand deposits in savings accounts, instruments payable on demand, etc. Property is also shares of stock representing equity ownership in an enterprise; it is the paid-up value of a life insurance policy, an annuity for retirement, a right under a contract, a franchise, a guarantee or any other mature vested interest that gives the individual owner the right to command certain goods or services in support of his liberty.

The Conservative is profoundly concerned with the preservation of all existing property rights and is directly interested in the conversion of certain benefits, privileges, and quasi-contractual rights into mature vested property rights that can be asserted with the full force of law. We have considered, under the discussion of mobility, the matter of employment "fringe benefits." An associated interest that should be converted to a mature and vested right, at the earliest date possible, is the Social Security benefit.

The system of social welfare issuing from the Social Security Act is the source of much concern to the Conservative. This does not mean that the Conservative neither believes it feasible nor desirable to systematically provide social insurance for the temporarily underemployed or the unemployable by reason of age or disability. The apprehensions arise from the defects that inhere in the existing act. These involve great dangers to the American society and body politic.

The Social Security Act, as amended in 1939 and subsequently, provides for a compulsory pension system for disabled and former retired workers and spouses paid for by taxes levied on all active workers subject to the act. The plan in this respect constitutes no more or less than enforced contribution from the employed to the retired, regardless of need.

The life insurance system consists of taxes levied on all workers subject to the act regardless of dependent status and payable to the survivors of deceased workers regardless of need. This is nothing more or less than compulsory life insurance.

Unemployment compensation provides for partial federal supervision and control over the state-operated systems where all employees subject to the act are forced to contribute to unemployed workers regardless of need.

As a last feature of the system, provision is made for contributions to state-operated programs for maternal and child health, child welfare, and crippled children.

There are those non-Conservatives among us who would rewrite history to read that charity, Christian charity was never a feature of Western civilization until the benevolent Social Security Act was passed in the depths of the Great Depression. This is, of course, a bold distortion designed to divert and not answer the critics of the present compulsory system. The facts are that Western society has long accepted the idea that aid to those without means is a general social burden. Prior to the growth of the modern state, this burden was assumed by the religious institution, the worker's guild, or the lord of the manor.

Government is the logical successor to these historical agencies. In the modern industrial state, only the government embraces the whole of the society and is thus capable of distributing the cost of the burden to those who will bear it.

The background to the present social-welfare system can be traced to the national insurance scheme advanced by Bismarck in 1881. The Social Security system first successfully instituted in Germany was followed by similar systems in most other Western nations.

It was only after the character of American opportunity changed with the settlement of the West that significant agitation developed in the United States for compulsory insurance and pension measures similar to those adopted in Europe. Despite some flirtation by the States with pension schemes, it was not until the middle of the Great Depression that the general public came to accept the idea.

The present scheme of Social Security followed experiments with federal assistance to the states through Reconstruction Finance Corporation Loans and the WPA relief agency.

Despite the great pressure for hurried enactment, the original plan provided for a self-supporting system. This was abandoned in 1939 by amendment when a trust fund without actuarial basis was substituted for the Reserve account. All pretense of insurance on a contributing basis was abandoned in favor of a compulsory tax-supported welfare system.

Although the original act was amended many times, no substantial changes were effected until 1950. At this time, action was taken to liberalize eligibility requirements, extend coverage, and provide supplementary benefits to the families of the retired or deceased worker. All amendments since 1950 have been of this character, working toward wider participation and more liberal benefit treatment.

Despite all of the amendments, the act still provides for a compulsory federal system of pension and life insurance and grants-in-aid to states for social welfare purposes.

It is impossible to predict the future of the system. At this writing, great political pressure is being asserted to attach a compulsory medical benefit scheme. This plan would conform to the prevailing theory of compulsory participation with a tax levied on the active worker to disburse benefits to the retired.

One feature is clear, however. Unless there is a basic change in the underlying concept, members of the working population will continue to be forced to contribute to the incomes of the retired without regard to the latter's need.

The defenders of the prevailing system would have us believe that the act benefits the needy as well as those without substantial need, but this does not hold up under analysis. In fact, only those with substantial resources of their own are in a position to retire and thereby become eligible for the benefit. There are few citizens who can retire and live on their Social Security pension alone. As the cost of living increases, as our needs expand as a people, the number who can retire on their Social Security pension alone will diminish accordingly. The benefits of the act are anticipated to become increasingly devoted to those who have ample retirement funds of their own.

From the point of view of those who are for any reason unable to accumulate independent resources to sustain themselves in retirement, Social Security is but a cruel hoax. They will work all of their productive lives paying compulsory taxes to supplement the retirement income of the affluent, the independent, and then upon reaching the age of sixty-five, be forced to continue working and contributing to the retirement income of those favored citizens to whom Social Security is but a supplement.

Where is the social justice in a system that purports to be "an act to provide for the general welfare . . ." and works to compel the less affluent, the less favored, to contribute to supplement the retired income of the affluent, the favored, the rich, the persons of independent means?

The entire welfare aspect of this program is inconsistent with the basic Conservative position. The very fact that the benefits are paid out of current tax revenues, and thus the plan is not funded on a sound fiscal basis, opens up the whole system to bureaucratic abuse. The beneficiaries of the plan do not receive a vested interest in the balance of their account at any time. The amount of the benefit and the eligibility criteria are always subject to legislative revision. And another principal Conservative objection to the program is the fact that it is discriminatory. The concept of "equal opportunity for all to acquire property" is violated through the multiple restrictions and deficiencies of the system.

Conservative reform of the system would require first of all that the plan be placed upon a sound fiscal basis; that it be funded; and that the property so entrusted to the care of the agency be administered with fidelity and respect. The system would be converted from just another bureau disbursing tax revenues to a select group of individuals into a responsible administrative agency functioning as the custodian of the participants' property. All of the highly developed protections applicable to trusteeship would operate to protect the beneficial interests. All discrimination as to eligibility would be eliminated immediately. Eligibility would be extended to all without regard to source of income or other limitations. Each participant would have the opportunity to purchase the maximum benefit available. Economic class distinctions would have no place in the system.

Along with the limitation of discriminatory restrictions on eligibility would be a removal of the compulsory feature. The non-Conservative argument that some persons just aren't responsible and won't provide for their old age unless they are compelled to do so by a benevolent but despotic government is just as opposed to Conservative concepts of liberty here as anywhere else. Not only are such actions unsound and inconsistent with liberty but also, to a considerable extent, disruptive of Conservative society. Prohibition was a clear example of the extreme application of this type of "we know better than you what is good for you" reasoning.

The destructive aspect of the compulsion within the Social Security system is not as dramatic as the reaction to the Volstead Act, but it is there nevertheless. All one needs do is to consider the sad plight of the aged, who have been led to believe, by this benevolent despotic system, that Social Security will take care of them in their old age. Many are prevented from retiring from their jobs because inflation has made the "benefit" inadequate to sustain them.

If Social Security is welfare and charity, let it be honestly identified as such, but if it is a right, then let it become a full-fledged property right enforceable in any court of law. Let there be no restrictions to the "annuity" income contingent on earnings. It is a typically non-Conservative concept to force an otherwise productive individual into retirement at some arbitrary age or seduce him into idleness by the promise of a little reward.

Destructive to character is the necessity to rationalize to one's self that the benefit check is just getting back what the recipient put in. The basic fallacy of this assertion is so apparent that the individual must intentionally blind himself to facts in order to arrive at this conclusion. Under the influence of this system, the senior citizen, who has really earned a right to the dignity of this elder role, is robbed of his independence and forced into a delinquent condition of self-deception or worse malefaction.

The Conservative accepts the essential virtue of a system of social insurance but without approving of a compulsory general tax-supported welfare system, without regard to need. In the absence of a suitable alternative and in advance of substantial experience, the present system has been useful. It is now time to transform this system to one with attributes that will work to preserve the dignity of the individual and to sustain his liberty, his essential independence in his declining years.

If immediate conversion to a full status is impractical, a phased conversion at least is indicated. At the very minimum, all persons under forty years of age should be placed on a fully funded basis at once. Their accounts would be vested without delay. Participation would be unlimited as to source and amount of income. Participation could be permitted to make the entire premium payment individually or to negotiate with their employer to have the entire payment made from retained earnings. Compulsion should be completely removed, with perhaps a tax credit as an inducement.

All that would remain, to sustain the integrity of the system, would be for the government to keep faith and forever reject the policy of currency debasement. Each participant then could confidently look forward to a period of retirement from his toil, where the natural advances in productivity to which he contributed so much during his productive years, will mean that the dollars he receives will have more and not less power to command the things he needs to sustain himself and those dependent on him.

Security lies at the base of the realization of a condition of liberty. Security means that capacity to command resources to one's own use in sufficient quantities to avoid a dependent status. Dependency is the direct antithesis of liberty. Compulsory schemes of retained earnings, deferred compensation, and welfare systems all contribute to the development of a dependency status that is destructive of liberty. Destruction of liberty creates a static condition of regimentation. Spontaneity is thereby eliminated as a characteristic of social behavior—stagnation and decline ensue.

The alternative to stagnation is constructive development arising out of the unregulated and uninhibited relationship of individuals in the pursuit of their self-interest within an ordered society. This is predicated upon the essence of a Conservative society characterized by the maximum mobility in the individual to pursue his development as he sees it.

SECURITY AND CONSERVATION OF THE STATE

The imperative that is common to all roles of government is the security and conservation of the state.

The roles of government, consistent with the Conservative position, are those traditional functions associated with the policing of the society such that the maximum liberty is realizable by all, and each is protected in the exercise of his inalienable rights; the administration of justice such that each individual is so protected in his person and property that he is not exposed unassisted to irreparable harm or denied redress where protection from exposure is inappropriate; the faithful administration of the functions entrusted to its care, in the public interest, with the understanding that the public interest never transcends one individual's right[66] and the function of providing for the common defense.

Under the terms of the Constitution, the birth certificate of the Federal Republic, the central government has the exclusive responsibility to provide for the conduct of all relations with foreign states and to provide for the defense of the nation. The conduct of foreign affairs and the providing for the national defense are companion roles so interrelated that they are subject to but one evaluation, the security interests of the citizen and the state.

Clausewitz said, "War is but diplomacy carried on by other means." Winston Churchill is quoted as saying that "We arm to parley." The substance of both of these observations is that a nation that lacks the strength to protect cannot hope to prosecute its interests.

Social order is coercive order. Where there is not a strong marshal, all citizens must go armed. The most peaceable must necessarily carry a weapon with the ability and disposition to use it so that the potentially violent will be encouraged toward rational and restrained behavior.

The United States exists in a world community of national states, where national interest, as the power elite of each conceives it, is the guide to national action. As an incipient poison corroding the life substance of all peoples of the world is the international or nonnational Communist conspiracy. In such an environment, there is but one reliable guide to the conduct of a national foreign policy—the consistent defense of the nation's security interests. Does the action or inaction serve the basic security interests of the nation, and the millions of American citizens? This is the only reliable and legitimate guide.

Those security interests of the American people can be successfully prosecuted only after those interests are clearly identified and understood. Once identified and understood, the assignment of related priorities is indispensable.

The Conservative knows that the American people occupy the lonely position at the very front from the march of Western civilization. The column stretches far into antiquity beyond the Greek City States and the Golden Age of Pericles. The beginning was before Moses and included the enlightened Egyptian Pharaoh Akhenaton with his loving god. The solitude of the American people is the solitude of leadership, of being the willing, even eager heirs to the most fruitful and yet promising civilization mankind has developed.

The American people are as a relay runner who has been passed the baton of liberty. Should their step falter, drop the baton, and be compelled to halt and retrieve, the forces of reaction surely will overtake them only to be overcome at a far greater expenditure of energy.

This revolution, to which we are heir, began when the first slave was set free from his condition of servitude. In this race, the laurels of victory will only crown mankind in a gold age, where liberty will be universally accepted as man's natural condition. Never must we be diverted from the stark reality that the forces of counterrevolution and reaction are but one step behind. We will be sustained in our struggle by our faith in the assurance of the victory of liberty over tyranny and darkness. The critical issue to keep forever before us is the fact that so long as one remains to be set free, the freedom of all who walk free remains threatened.

The transcendent interest of each American is liberty, nothing less. Any action of the servants of the American people that is inconsistent with this security interest is counter to the basic interest. The American government has the power but never the right to compromise the basic interest of those from whom it derives its just powers.

The federal government can have no super allegiance to the United Nations, nor can it have any responsibility to any other sovereignty. It can engage in international arrangements and associations only where the interest of liberty of the American people is served.

National independence cannot be substituted for liberty, and the responsibility cannot be escaped through the catch phrase of "nonintervention" in the internal affairs of another state.

The American people have a permanent interest in the condition of liberty of all mankind. Their government is obliged to employ the power entrusted to it to intervene in or otherwise influence the condition of liberty wherever man dwells. Our only permanent alliance is with the force of liberty; all others are marriages of convenience.

The non-Conservative might tell us that the government must remain free to maneuver, compromise, and cleverly advance the interests of the United States, and must not be hampered by inconvenient restrictions. The Conservative answers: liberty is not an ideal to be pursued but the natural condition of man. To frustrate liberty will contain forces that will ultimately break forth with convulsive and often uncontrollable force. Foreign and security policies can compromise with "reaction and counterrevolution" for the transient illusion of success only in exchange for the certainty of ultimate violent and perhaps catastrophic failure.

America must not seek to turn the head of the column, go back and join the "reliable" wagons following behind, form a circle, and seek to defend what has already been won against the onslaught of hostile forces of reaction and counterrevolution. The annals of history are filled with accounts of peoples who were engulfed by the forces of barbarism that stormed their walls. Liberty is not to be secured in static defenses. El Dorado remains beyond the mountains. Press on, we must. We stand now where the vanguard of the advance has always stood, on the frontier.

It does not follow that alliances with other states are undesirable, but all alliances must be recognized for what they are. An alliance does not become a partnership by calling it such. It does not create a community simply by labeling it as such. It does not become synonymous with the cause of liberty by likening it to a "brotherhood of freedom-loving peoples." Liberty remains liberty, and we dare not retreat from our position of leadership to take even temporary refuge in compromise association with those whom we must lead. Had we been entirely clear on this matter, many of our costly mistakes of the past fifty years might have been avoided.

The non-Conservative has a tendency of going about calling up grand but illusory phrases as a substitute for the real interest, liberty. President Wilson led the nation to war to "make the world safe for democracy." President Roosevelt conceived of the "Four Freedoms" and proclaimed freedom from want and fear as objectives. President Truman propelled the nation to war to "save the United Nations and contain Communist aggression." The Conservative knows that not one of the wars was fought for an objective worth the shedding of one drop of American blood. This is not to say that the wars were avoidable or were conducted badly from a military standpoint. This is beyond the scope of this consideration. What is meant is that not one of these political objectives was anything but fantasy and myth.

These observations will offend the unduly sentimental, but just a quick consideration of the manner in which the interests of the American people were served flowing out of the interventions compels the conclusion. The proof of the pudding is not on the outside of the package. It is as it has always been, in the eating. The non-Conservative might suggest that it was not the glorious objectives that were faulty, but the sinister workings of reaction that frustrated their realization after the forces of evil had been defeated. This is apologetic nonsense. It was the objectives that were faulty because they were unreal, not in accordance with the underlying current of man's development. This is why they were so fragile as to founder and break up on the first barrier reef to be encountered as they approached the shore.

The nobility of the aims of Wilson's fourteen points, the Four Freedoms, and the Atlantic Charter of Roosevelt, and the United Nations that Truman sought to preserve are not the question. It is lack of reality which is the weakness.

Remember well. The aftermath of World War I was the rise of Hitler, Mussolini, Tojo, and other lesser practitioners of the black art of government based upon terror and brutality. Communism rose to a position of power in the aftermath of this crusade to become, under Stalin, the enemy of all liberty.

World War II saw the defeat of the forces of Nazism, Fascism, and Japanese militarism. The tragic aftermath was to deliver into bondage more individuals than had been set free. Where the forces of Nazism, Fascism, and militarism receded from Eastern Europe and Asia, the darkness of Communism descended like an inky cloud, exuded from some gigantic squid to obscure all light in the land.

Only a habituated idealistic dreamer could now hold out the remotest hope for the United Nations as it was originally conceived. The grand design predicated on the myth of "four-power cooperation" has become what it was destined to become from the beginning: a "tower of Babel" on the East River. When the UN failed to come to the aid of those who were butchered by Communism in Hungary and Tibet, but bravely employed Canberra jet bombers against poorly equipped and scarcely trained Africans in their Katanga homes, it revealed its inert form as an instrument of justice among men. It has been revealed for what it is, a disorganized, nonprincipled institution capable of employing any means to accomplish some non-Conservative utopian end.

General Wedemeyer once observed in substance that the very heart of the grand strategy is to stay out of wars that one doesn't have to get into, and from which there is something to be gained by staying out. In 1914, the prosecution of the strategic interests of the United States was related to the expanse of the Atlantic, the Monroe Doctrine, and the British Navy. These three factors combined to shield the United States from aggressive interference by foreign powers. If the diminishing ability of the British Navy to sweep the seas clean of the German U-boats constituted a significant threat to the United States, the nation was justified in intervention so far as was necessary to protect the interest threatened. This did not justify in any way the blood sacrifice of American youth on the altar of the non-Conservative myth of "Save the World for Democracy." The retreat of the American people into isolation following World War I, in no small measure, reflects the shock they felt at the exposure of the falsity of the god.

Without here debating again the question of culpability by the non-Conservative Roosevelt Administration for the conduct of affairs leading up to "Pearl Harbor," in fact, the prosecution of World War II became a confusion of the non-Conservative mythology of "unconditional surrender," "four-power cooperation," the "Morgenthau Plan" for postwar Germany, the Atlantic Charter, and the Four Freedoms. The United Nations was constructed on the very foundation of the grand myth, four-power cooperation. Countless American youths were again slaughtered on blood-soaked beaches, shell-torn fields, or committed to watery graves in the service of these non-Conservative myths. The fundamental failure was again what it had been in World War I; the failure to clearly identify the real security interests of the American people.

Toward the close of World War II, all possibility of salvaging the real security interest of the American people was sacrificed by the non-Conservatives in a dream of "one world" based upon the fantasy of four-power cooperation. This myth, which formed the very foundation of the dream edifice, was shattered in the immediate postwar period by the trenchant actions of Communism, but dreams die hard.

In Korea, the non-Conservative Truman administration committed thousands of American youths to solitary deaths in a far-off land in order to seek to breathe life into the corpse that but needed to be decently interred. The idea that Korea was not vital to the United States' strategic security interests was asserted by no less a person than the Secretary of State, Dean Acheson,[67] shortly before the North Korean forces moved across the thirty-eighth Parallel. The only plausible reasons that President Truman could have had were to pursue the myth of "containment" and attempt to revive the dying body of the United Nations. If there was any question of the fact that it was the myth of the four-power cooperation that had given the United Nations an appearance of life in the beginning, first Tibet and then Hungary in 1956, exposed the putrefying, rotting, and indecently uninterred corpse for what is was, stillborn. The United Nations does not now and never has had the capacity to solve the basic political problems that were simply locked in the closet at San Francisco.

President Washington cautioned in the earliest days of the infant nation: "It is our true policy to steer clear of permanent alliances with any portion of the foreign world".[68] It could be only suggested by one completely unfamiliar with the wisdom of this great soldier and statesman that President Washington was suggesting that the United States should retreat behind some static wall of defense and decline participation in the affairs of the world. What he was recognizing was the fact that the United States' interests are the interests of the American people and that their government was obliged to remain unentangled in static international relationships to remain free to prosecute those interests.

General George Washington was a towering Conservative who understood the reliable constants in society and the life of a nation, the constants of change. The environment within which a people live is in a constant state of flux, and only that government will be capable of conserving the basic interests of the people, which retains the greatest capacity to respond to the shifting forces that threaten their interests.

The non-Conservative is constantly prevented from seeing the world for what it is because his vision is obscured by his mythology of what ought to be. Because of this mythical conception of the environment within which the non-Conservative operates, reality has the constant unsettling effect of intruding upon the dreams. The skeletons keep popping out of the closet. The consequence is not to awaken the non-Conservative from his fantasy but to propel him into sort of a comatose state where his fixations become real, and immune from the unsettling reality. "Myth-think" becomes the characteristic reasoning processing in his schizophrenic flight, and he becomes obsessed with the institutionalization of human relationships. Only here can he take refuge from the disturbing condition of change. Once constructed, the institution becomes the substitute for reality and then all can be justified in the defense of the institution with its noble purposes. The end becomes the defense of the institution, and any means will be justified to secure this end. All of the justification lies in the grand design of the institution itself.⁶⁹

Detailed consideration of the conduct of affairs relating to United States security interests demonstrates that the non-Conservative is just not equipped by disposition, or comprehension, to be the reliable guardian of the interests. He is psychologically unsuited to the task, as the long line of failures will attest.

It is not accidental that non-Conservative administrations wage two world wars for myths and illusory dreams, and the Korean "police action" to attempt to breathe life into the dead and decaying body of the UN. These were adventures that conform to the non-Conservative schizophrenia thought processes. Neither was it accidental that the conservatively influenced Eisenhower administration avoided such adventures for eight long years, and that within one year following the introduction of the non-Conservative Kennedy Administration, there has been an abortive participation in a revolutionary invasion of Communist Cuba, and the United States support of the UN to wage war in the Congo. (Note: while the Eisenhower Administration authorized USAF airlift to the Congo, it never authorized airlift within the Congo in support of military operations.) The last-minute decision to withdraw air support from the tiny force in the Bay of Pigs and thus condemn the little rebel band, was entirely that of President Kennedy. Memory is disturbed by the similarity of this action of the Red Army at the gates of Warsaw in 1944. There the signal was given for the non-Communist Underground to rise up. The Red Army then sat on its hands while they (the non-Communist Underground) were liquidated by the German forces. Following the liquidation, the Red Army moved on the city and drove out the Wehrmacht. Polish Communists moved in with the Red Army. Poland is a Communist satellite today.

There is little hope that meddling intervention and involvement in international visionary schemes grounded in myth will cease until the prosecution of the security interests of the American people rests again reliably in Conservative hands.

Plaintive non-Conservative cries should be anticipated to follow from any critical appraisal of the UN. Once again, the shout will be raised that "the Conservative is even against the UN" and cries of "isolationist" will follow. To submit the institution of the UN to comparative analysis alongside the basic security interests of the American people is to attack the grandest icon of them all, and this is unforgivable to the non-Conservative Liberal mind. Of course, to suggest that the Conservative is against the UN is just pure nonsense, but the indictment is soul satisfying to the Liberal because it is all but equal in his mind to say that the Conservative is against motherhood and a full dinner pail. Frightening is the irrational tenacity with which the cherished illusion is held of the UN based upon the mythological concept of four-power cooperation.

The Conservative looks upon the UN as he looks upon all international institutions. It is an institution, which is subject to all of the frailties and defects characteristic of institutions in general. It has a tendency to become inflexible, unresponsive, and preoccupied with the advancement of its own vested interests. The institution can be relied upon to develop institutionalized interests that are contrary to and actively oppose the basic interests of those it purports to serve. The UN is particularly susceptible to the latter characteristic because its fundamental constituent membership embraces all varieties of political positions from governments controlled by militant international communists, socialists, fascists and military dictatorships, and feudal monarchies to constitutional republics.

The Conservative understands that the United States is the most advanced and enlightened of all the constituent political institutions. This fact alone foreordains that the basic interests of the UN and the United States will conflict. Where those interests do conflict, the United States government has no other Constitutional course but to prosecute the interests of the United States independent of those of the UN. To remain in a position to assert and prosecute the interests of the United States, our participation within the UN must always remain conditional and dynamic, never conceived as permanent, fixed, or static.

The question can legitimately be raised here as to how we, as inhabitants upon this planet, are ever to achieve a wider political association within which to prosecute the fundamental interest—liberty? The Conservative answer is that the torch of liberty has not been passed into our hands by a wishful and visionary predecessor. It was surrendered reluctantly and grudgingly into hands that reached out and seized the torch. We shall not surrender the torch except to hands that are stronger, firmer, and more eager to accept the leadership than we are to retain it. Only in this way can we comfortably accept the lead of another and devote our energies in following, supporting, and sustaining. The lead must be wrested from our hands by a force that demonstrates through the seizure the capacity to hold and press on.

This then is the Conservative answer to those who assert that the UN represents the last hope of peace, of progress, of liberty, and freedom of mankind. The Conservative says to such dispirited Americans, you have lost your perspective in the illusion of a world, which is unity. The world and mankind is not just divided but is fractioned. This is the reality with which we must deal.

The United States stands today where it has always stood, alone in a hostile world. The United States strides into the future as a solitary figure. This has been characteristic of its condition since birth in 1776. With our faith in God, confidence in our destiny, assurance in our ability, and the steadfast courage and patience to discharge our responsibility as we see it, it is our mission to lead mankind to a free and enlightened tomorrow.

Recognition of the fact of solitary leadership, which is our role, means that we must introduce ourselves and our influence into all of the affairs of mankind and the nations of the world. We can decline to participate only at the cost of surrendering our leadership to hands less reliable than our own. Our role is both our burden and our opportunity to carry on the civilizing process, which has seen mankind progress from a condition little above that of the beast to enlightenment and promise. Ours is the inheritance of Akhenaton, Heraclitus, Moses, Socrates, Christ, and St. Paul. We are the heirs of St. Augustine, Aquinas, Goethe, Coke, Bacon, Nietzsche, and Shakespeare. Euclid, Pythagoras, Galileo, da Vinci, Newton, and Einstein are our ancestors. We are, at once, the link with the past and the bridge to the future. Justice Oliver Holmes, Jr., said it well in 1884: "As life is action and passion, it is required of a man that he should share the passion and action of his time, at the peril of being judged not to have lived." Let not future generations of historians record that in the mid-twentieth century, there was a people who had the responsibilities of leadership and greatness within their grasp and that they shrank from the action and passion of their time. Let not the judgment of history be that we dared not and did not therefore live.

It is our role and our duty to be the architect of alliances among nations for the purpose of advancing the condition of liberty throughout the world. We are obliged by our position as a nation to participate in and influence the course of regional arrangements that promise to advance the condition or fashion the environment within which man will be encouraged to advance his condition of liberty. We must withhold our participation or withdraw from and otherwise actively oppose those associations that tend toward the destruction of liberty or the environment within which liberty advances. It is on this basis and this basis alone, that the Conservative appraises our participation in North Atlantic Treaty Organization, the Organization of American States, the Alliance for Progress, Southeast Asia Treaty Organization, the International Monetary Fund, and all other international arrangements.

Never should we convey the understanding to an ally that we are participating on any other basis than the basis that the advancement of liberty throughout all mankind is the fundamental and permanent strategic interest of the American people, and consequently, their government is without legitimate authority to depart from the active prosecution of this end.

Understanding of the basic American strategic interest and its relationship to the role of leadership of the American people is of particular significance when applied to what is commonly referred to as "foreign aid." Several months after assuming the responsibilities for the direction of all foreign aid activities under the new Economic Cooperation Administration, Mr. Fowler Hamilton appears on the television program *Meet the Press*. In answer to a question posed by Mr. Spivak, relative to the approach that his administration was going to take to the administration of aid (grants or loans), Mr. Hamilton responded to the effect that he had instructed his subordinates to ask the preliminary question, was the aid in the fundamental interest of the United States? He then went on to indicate his conception of this fundamental interest, as our interest in strengthening countries that are independent. Mr. Hamilton described the basic criterion for granting the aid as whether it was likely to strengthen independence. President Kennedy emphasized this point of view in the State of the Union address in 1962, where he positively expressed the interest of the United States as limited to the independence of the state.[70]

The Conservative responds to this conception of the basic interests of the American people by a complete rejection of the asserted validity of the idea. The national independence of a particular state has only Conservative significance if it corresponds to a domestic condition of individual liberty within that state. The American people have no interest in reinforcing the yoke of despotism and subjugation around the necks of any people. Our treasure is not legitimately exported to assist some authoritarian regime to forge chains with which to shackle its subjects into a condition of dependent servitude.

There are some conceivable circumstances where the tactical interest of the United States might be served by supplying crisis aid to a Communist, Fascist, Socialist, or other authoritarian or totalitarian regime, but the aid would have to be reconciled with the strategic interest as well, with the full understanding that in the long run, it must work toward the extension of the condition of liberty to accord with the basic interests of the American people.

Aid to the Socialist Congress Party of Nehru's India should be recognized as contributing to a condition in which liberty is prejudiced. Aid to Ghana should be viewed as helping to sustain a regime inimical to liberty. Aid to Communist Yugoslavia and Poland can be considered no more than expedient. The circumstances under which aid would be made available to a nation, such as Egypt, which had embarked upon the destructive course of expropriation, would have to be unique and pressing.

In each instance, the evaluation must be made as to whether the condition of liberty promises to be advanced more fruitfully through the extension or the withholding of the aid. It is not pertinent, when appraising the interest of the American people that the aid is in the form of grants or repayable loans. The United States government is not in the business of making commercial loans, and thus all aid must be assessed against the strategic and tactical interests.

Once it has been decided that the aid promises to advance the condition of liberty, the further question must be answered: can we afford the exportation of treasure?

If the exportation tends to undermine our economic strength, this must be realistically faced and not just dismissed by the resort to some myth about our national affluence and the observations that nothing must be spared. We must recognize that the role that we have accepted leads down a long and difficult path. We will need all of our strength for the journey. The forces arrayed against us are immense. We must be hard-headed and practical and expend our precious energies and resources wisely. Prolificacy could be our undoing. We cannot indulge in delusions of grandeur. We must conserve and never squander our precious resources.

Often we hear the catchy phrase, "Trade, not aid." This slogan, like most, is an oversimplification of a rather complex idea that contains within it an element of truth.

We, in these United States, understand the relationship of the private ownership of property to the condition of individual liberty. The Conservative knows that individual liberty will remain stillborn or wither where private ownership of property is denied by a society through its governing authority. The Conservative recognizes that wherever man has not yet achieved liberty, has achieved a condition of liberty and lost it, or where his present condition of liberty is threatened, the basic interests of the American people are threatened. The Conservative asserts that wherever private ownership of property is denied or threatened, the same basic interests of the American people are threatened. It is the security of these interests, which it is the responsibility of the government to defend and extend.

Where a society, through its government, petitions the American people through their government, to grant them assistance in dealing with a particular set of economic circumstances, preliminary questions should be asked by the representatives of the American people on their behalf. The United States government should ask of the foreign government, "What have your people done to help themselves in this matter in which you seek now the aid of those we represent?"

The government representative must first determine that the petitioning people have sought to employ the private capital resources available, and the application was either unavailable or inappropriate under the existing circumstances. At a minimum, the petitioning government would be required to satisfy the United States government that the petitioning government has not avoided private financing because of any dogmatic or doctrinaire attitude in opposition to the private ownership of property secured under the general operation of a system of law. Any history of expropriation of property interests for which just compensation had not been tendered the rightful owners would place the petitioner automatically on the ineligible list.

The Conservative understands that it is through the private exportation of capital by American investors in foreign enterprises that fundamental alliances are forged in pursuit of the basic interest of the American people. Where working associations are created in foreign nations between the representatives of American owners of private property and nationals of the foreign state, the condition of liberty is advanced. It is not through the few representatives of the federal bureaucracy dealing with the governmental representatives of a foreign state that the fullest liberating force and influence of the American people is asserted.

It is through the thousands of Americans doing business throughout all the remote corners of the world, in the pursuit of opportunities to employ American capital productively and profitably, that reliable relationships are created. The partnership relationships so created are not based upon the fragile foundation of foreign aid, with its implication of princely dispensation of largess to the pauper. Partners in business retain their dignity, for the profits that accrue to their interests are the earnings of their sweat and just reward.

The Conservative conceives of government-to-government aid as a useful tool of international policy but never as the main source of American foreign investment or other export of capital. Government-to-government aid is not the type of aid that can be relied upon to form the sound basis for economic development. If the basic environment is there and the conditions exist that are receptive to the constructive employment of such aid, some rather startling results can be anticipated, as in Europe and the Marshall Plan. Where the requisites for free economic activity based upon a system of law, securing the private ownership of property and relying upon competition and the marketplace mechanism are absent, then the aid can be viewed as but an expedient to get the people over a particularly rough winter, as it were. This is the basis for disaster relief, crisis assistance, but never investment with the objective of some permanent gain.

If the government-to-government aid tends to subsidize a political elite in a position of power that it would be unable to sustain in the absence of the aid, the additional question is asked by the Conservative, "Is it in the interests of the American people to intercede on behalf of the existing government and shield it from its own political realities?"

If the power elite support the requisite institutions that facilitate a prevailing condition of liberty, it may be in the interests of the American people to advance the aid. If, however, the power elite are unreceptive or opposed to the development of the requisite institutions, it then stands opposed to the basic interests of the American people and thus should not be subsidized with their treasure, except for other compelling reasons.

The non-Conservative has a rather deceptive tendency to acknowledge the role of international business and investment by the millions of individual Americans as a sort of partnership with the federal bureaucracy in some grand design. We are told that the federal government recognizes the partnership role of private capital in the field of foreign economic development. It is long past time that the power-grabbing bureaucrat was forcibly reminded of the position that he occupies within our society. He is the servant of the people, and the people are not some great collective entity in the Marxian sense but 180 million plus individual free American citizens. The federal government exists for the single legitimate purpose, to serve the interests of those same 180 million individual Americans and the Commonwealth in which they reside.

As servant of the people, the federal government cannot, under any circumstances, enter into a partnership relationship with them in the usual sense of the word. The very meaning of partnership comprehends an association between equals. The essence of the relationship is that each assumes the same degree of liability for the debts of the enterprise. Sovereignty itself precludes the fact of equality. The federal government derives its sovereignty from the consent of the governed, the people, and has no sovereign existence independent of them. With respect to liability, it is the people who are liable for all of the debts that they incur as individuals and for all those debts incurred on their behalf by their government as their servant.

The responsibility of the federal government is to extend all appropriate assistance and protection to American citizens who go abroad seeking opportunities to transact business and otherwise invest in offshore economic enterprises. The responsibility to accord equal opportunity to all is just as binding on the extranational activities of American citizens as it is in relation to their exclusively domestic activities.

Equality of opportunity applies to all of the activities of the individuals and does not admit of exceptions. Foreign and domestic economic activities are not legitimately divided one from another, and the one discriminated against in favor of another. Foreign aid is not appropriately employed in such a manner that otherwise promising opportunities for foreign investment by private capital is usurped by government planners. Wherever a particular opportunity is presented for the loan of capital, the direct investment and the participation in the activity or the contracting of a service, the foreign petitioning people should be encouraged to seek private participation.

When considering the matters relating to foreign aid and private investment abroad, one comes face-to-face with questions of international "balance of payments" and their connection to the United States gold reserve, potential expropriation, tariffs, quotas, and other barriers to inhibit trade. Each of these subjects could provide material for a book length exploration to consider them in their technical depth. We shall not attempt any such profound treatment here, but a few observations with respect to each are appropriate.

When we talk of international balance of payments, we are really talking about the continued capacity of the American people to discharge their role of leadership in Western civilization, nothing less. The gold supply that we own as a people is the discipline mechanism behind the United States dollar. In effect, if the discipline mechanism is destroyed, the dollar becomes, in fact, a monetary unit without discipline. Money without discipline will quickly lose the confidence of the millions of people throughout the world, and from that day forward, the American people and their government will find it most difficult to exercise effective influence. It is the integrity of our dollar which is, more than anything else, the bellwether of the confidence the world has in us as a people. If the dollar falters, other currencies based to a large extent on the dollar falter also.

An undisciplined dollar means a political dollar. This will tend to command less and less in the world markets. Each time we try to invest, we will find it will take many more dollars to do the job, or the host will simply ask for some other currency such as the German mark, the British pound, the French franc, or the USSR ruble. The dollar must be kept disciplined and sound lest the security of the American people be threatened.

Where there exists a net imbalance of payments resulting in increasing the claims against our gold reserves to a point where the discipline mechanism is threatened, there are at least two possible alternatives. The federal government may elect to cut back on the exportation of capital through foreign aid, or the government may act to restrict the private export of investment and other capital. The Conservative position would weigh heavily in favor of first restricting government-to-government aid, recognizing that long-term investment with the anticipated profit return feature characteristic of private exportation works to sustain liberty.

Under a policy of encouraging, through nondiscrimination, noninterference, and private investment abroad, the problem of expropriation by the host government must be considered. The United States government cannot just adopt a policy of noninterference with and encouragement of the private investment in foreign lands and then wash its hands of the whole affair. American citizens and their interests are entitled to the protection of their government no matter where they are situated. This does not mean, however, that a particular financial interest should count on the American people coming to his embattled defense with a division of marines.

The Conservative conceives of the foreign exportation of capital as involving substantial risks, which must be assumed by the citizen investor. He knows that at least four parties must be satisfied with the beneficial aspects of the arrangement for it to succeed. The American investor must see a promise of profit. The United States government must not feel that the investment is contrary to the basic security interests of the American people. The nationals affected in the host country must see profit in the relationship, and finally, the host government must see the investment in its own interest. It is a fact that the host government can be substantially influenced in its judgment by the United States government, but this does not rule out the prospects of intervention or expropriation by the host government.

Many approaches have been suggested to this prevailing problem of the continuing threat of intervention or expropriation by foreign governments of American-owned assets in foreign lands. The great majority of suggestions that have been advanced seem to be either totally or partially non-Conservative in character. Most of the suggestions advanced by threatened business interests seem to either involve the intervention of the United States government or indemnification by the American people through their government for the loss sustained. It would seem that all faith is lost in the operation of the marketplace, and the competitive aspects of economics, with self-reliant acceptance of the inherent risks, just as soon as the sovereign border is reached. This seems to reflect but a weak attachment to the Conservative position and betrays a decided lack of imagination.

If we are to stand foursquare as the leader in man's struggle for liberty, we should not expose ourselves to the indictment that we believe in competition, individual self-reliance, and a realistic acceptance of the world as it is, only from the shelter of a privileged position. How much stronger would be our persuasive power in the dialogue with tyranny if Americans doing business abroad took the initiative in protecting themselves from routine hazards?

The mechanics of such protection are not as perplexing as those who run for cover under the federal umbrella would have us believe. The following suggestion might we worthy of exploration, at least before an otherwise enterprising businessman runs to Washington for help.

An international indemnification fund could be established on a premium basis with all participating business interests paying into the fund sums according to the risks involved in their particular operations.

The premium payments would be based upon the size of the interest insured and the risks to the interest. The premium paid by a business doing business in a country with a record of instability and expropriation would be substantially higher than would the premium paid to cover the same interest in a stable country with no such record.

If a loss is suffered by a particular interest through expropriation in country C for example, the premium rates for all other businesses doing business in that country would rise accordingly. The result would be to discourage the piecemeal expropriation that had been witnessed in the past.

The indemnified interest would transfer its recovery interest against the expropriating government to the fund that would then be subrogated to all of the rights of the indemnified interest against the offending government.

The size of the fund would be maintained at a level commensurate with all of the prevailing risks involved, and thus any substantial loss would cause a general rise in premium liability. This would work to take the profit out of participating businesses continuing to do business with the offending country following seizure.

After a certain point is reached in participation, the disadvantages of nonparticipation would be substantial. Any government that considered a plan of nationalization of foreign assets through expropriation would face the rather harsh fact that action against one interest would result in burdening the remaining interests to such an extent that their profits would be impaired; thus, the as-yet untouched interests would find it less desirable to continue in the old pattern. If the government contemplates general nationalization, it would find that a multitude of financial interests throughout the world would suffer by the loss and would thus be encouraged to take economic sanctions against the offending government. This could involve the denial of international credit facilities, transport, industrial maintenance, and resupply. To a considerable degree, an interest operating in a particular country and declining to participate would be inviting expropriation in advance of other protected interests.

The foregoing is not submitted as a detailed answer to the problem encountered in international or extranational enterprise but is submitted as a suggested area of study, which seems more in accord with the consistency of the Conservative position than does the reliance upon the government to pull the "chestnuts out of the fire." In another context, Mr. Truman made a remark that seems appropriate here. Mr. Truman said in effect that if one can't stand the heat, he should stay out of the kitchen.

Enterprise is always a gamble. The greater the risks undertaken, the greater should be the potential rewards or profits. We can respect the gambler or entrepreneur who prudently hedges his bets where appropriate, but it is most difficult to have respect for the loser who runs to the house to make good his losses. In this self-reliant way, the American entrepreneur who goes abroad would be saying to the world, "Look, we have come to you to work together for a more abundant future. We seek your cooperation and partnership in this greatest of all enterprises. We do not come as an arm of government, as the executor of a national policy. We come as individual Americans, dedicated to the principle of individual liberty, the dignity of each man and woman, and the reality that the condition of liberty lies within man's grasp."

If all of this is to have any meaning at all, if there is to be a bold assertion of leadership by the American people, we must adopt the spirit of the conqueror. We must approach our role as the custodians of the leadership of the Western civilization with a missionary zeal. If we are to say to our government, "Serve us, but do not rule us," we must each assert our leadership as individuals. Nothing less is our responsibility as a citizen of this republic.

We cannot logically and consistently say to our representatives, "Do not shift the burden from the back of the 'politically powerful' onto the backs of all the politically inarticulate and weak," and then say, "Protect me and what is mine from the risks of competition and the marketplace."

We cannot say to our government, "Withdraw from this business of foreign investment and business for this is not a legitimate role, but shield us from the competition of foreign enterprises." The Conservative belief in the validity of the marketplace mechanism cannot logically be confined to the nation's borders and held inapplicable once the border is crossed. If we believe in competition, then let us get into this thing of doing business and compete. The leaders of Western civilization should ask no quarter and give none.

The Conservative knows that competition strengthens, and the sheltering haven of privilege only makes he who is sheltered grow fat and phlegmatic. It has never made any real sense to strongly advocate the workings of the free market domestically and to seek controlled markets in foreign commerce. If the workings of the free market domestically tend to move the resources from the weaker to the stronger hands and to thus provide the maximum stimulus to abundance to sustain liberty, then protecting from foreign competition can only have the reverse effect of protecting the weak and thus retarding productive development.

How can the American businessman abroad be a persuasive leader in this struggle for liberty if he comes to the people of the foreign land and says to them, "I wish to be free to come here, but you are not free to go there (inside the United States)?" How can a less highly developed nation be persuaded of the economic power of a political system that must seek refuge from the competition of a low-wage economy? How much longer are we to allow the real image of leadership among us to be tarnished by the timid who only wish to wade and refuse to dive in where they must exert themselves to swim?

In the late months of 1961 and early 1962, we were presented with an approach to the matter of international business by many non-Conservatives. We were urged to give the federal bureaucracy the authority to negotiate general tariff reductions. The impetus behind this request was an alleged urgency to come to terms with what is commonly referred to as the European Common Market. We were told that we were faced with a whole new situation that requires urgent attention lest we be shut out of the great European market. The suggestion was made that if the federal government were not given this broad authority, that the European nations would turn protectionist against the United States and effectively shut us out of the market.

Generalizations of this nature are particularly difficult to substantiate. The fact of the matter is that marketing quotas are much more effective barriers to market access and these were to be generally reduced with respect to extra–Common Market producers. The fact that the Common Market would ultimately have a common external tariff did not mean that this would be higher than the individual tariffs were before. The fact was that the common external tariff would likely be lower than the prior prevailing average. To suggest that this great movement toward a free market, embracing substantially all of Europe, would all at once become protectionist in one of its major aspects did not seem coincident with the prevailing trends.

The Conservative would not argue that because the non-Conservative misread the true significance of the European Common Market, that the United States should not pay close attention to its import-export policies. Quite the reverse is the case. The case is even stronger for continuing reduction to final elimination of all barriers to trade not directly related to the bare essentials of military defense.

The true significance of the European Common Market is contained within the structural fact of the market itself and the promise of a substantial political union. The force of this economic-political concentration will indeed be something to reckon with. It is entirely possible that here will arise the vital force capable of wresting the leadership of Western civilization from the faltering grasp of the American people, who preferred the indulgent life of consumption to the vigorous and demanding life of leadership. Make no mistake. We will either lead or we will be led.

The compelling truth is that in the economic and then political unification of Europe, we are witnessing what promises to be a solution to the persistent tendency of Europe to wage what has amounted to recurring civil wars. These fratricidal adventures have sapped the European people of their vitality and denied them the leadership which was theirs. Finally, we have good reason to believe that after a number of false starts and detours into self-indulgent byways, the United States will get onto the main road and will press on in the quest for liberty.

Should Europe rise like the Phoenix from the ashes, stretch its mighty wings and soar above us all, we will have lost nothing, for us too will be carried aloft toward the millennium where liberty will be universally recognized as man's natural condition.

The Conservative rejects as timid, unimaginative, and unworthy of the people who lead the Western civilization, the non-Conservative posturings that we must join or come to terms with the "Common Market" lest we be shut out of the European market. This is the same kind of protectionist doctrine that is suited to a nation which is weak, immature, and struggling toward a position of power. This is not the reasoning which is characteristic of a people who are strong, dynamic, and vital; who know their role and are confident in their ability to meet their responsibilities of leadership.

Let us not go knocking on Europe's door with petty complaints of discrimination or preference. Let us not say to the representatives of the Common Market, "Permit us to keep our traditional share of your agriculture market." Europe is our competitor, not our master.

Let us rather say to our European brothers, cousins, aunts, and uncles, "We are delighted to see that you are doing so well. We have hoped all these years that we have encouraged you, and assisted you, that you would one day achieve this dynamic state. Now you are on your own. We have helped you bind your wounds, fed you nourishment during your recovery. This was our duty as your offspring and heir, but now the task is done. Rise now and walk alone. You will continue to receive our protection from those forces from which you are yet unable to protect yourself, but now you must face many of the risks on your own, for we will be occupied in our position as the leader and will not always be able to look back." Let us say to Europe, "Compete with us now in the market of the world."

Logic compels the Conservative to seek the dismantling of all sheltering devices that have tended to shield weak competitors and to perpetuate nonproductive economic conditions. Restrictions on imports of any kind, be they tariffs, quotas, or voluntary limitations by the exporting country tend to shield American business from the fact of competition. When our ears are offended by cries for protection from the managers of the steel companies or from the managers of the steel workers' union, we might conclude that the American people are just too weak to live in this world as free men. Is the American automobile industry so weak that there must be restrictions on the importation of foreign automobiles? What of farm products? Can we honestly say our agriculture is so nonproductive that we must limit the importation of foreign food stuffs? This is ridiculous. We are today the most productive people that have ever graced the face of the earth. We can compete successfully with any people anywhere, at any time, under any circumstances.

Let us now confront all the peoples of the world with our challenge. The Conservative who believes in the operation of the free competitive market mechanism would say, "We open our markets within the United States to your production without restriction; we ask only this of you in return, give us access to your market. We will not debate with you the merits of collective enterprise and individual subordination to the society, but we will demonstrate to you that private enterprise, based upon private ownership of property, secured by a rule of law, will produce abundance and facilitate liberty." What is needed is for us to practice what we preach and to pursue a planned dismantling of trade barriers throughout the world, but above all, let us dismantle our own.[71] The organization of international cooperation already exists in the General Agreement on Tariffs and Trade (GATT), and the United States is a leading member. Let us never lose sight of the fact that the Pacific as well as the Atlantic washes our shores, our interests circle the globe—run from the Arctic to the Antarctic and extend deep into space. The sky is no limit. Let us exercise our leadership in an arena consistent with our responsibilities and challenge Europe to compete.

The only legitimate use of trade barriers from the Conservative point of view should be to protect infant industry that would not be able to get underway otherwise and to conserve some essential military supply. This, of course, does not affect the legitimacy of the device of embargo and sanction in the pursuit of a tactical or strategic interest.

XI

THE SPECIAL PROBLEM OF THE COUNTERREVOLUTION[72]

The Conservative recognizes a whole variety of forces that are non-Conservative in character, which simply work to retard the advance of civilization through diversion of a people's productive energies or vitiation of their vitality and suppression of their dynamism. These forces are often far from harmless, to be sure, but generally, they can be dealt with in their turn through the standard techniques of exposure in the light of truth for the bankruptcy of their position. Occasionally, however, there arises a militant force of counterrevolution that threatens not to simply retard man's advance toward the society of liberty but threatens the very existence of the Conservative forces facilitating the advance. Today, we are confronted with just such a force of counterrevolution in military international socialism under the banner of Communism. This force has become institutionalized in the form of the international Communist conspiracy operating from the power base of the USSR dominating the Satellite-System, the Sino-Soviet alliance, and the international Communist party apparatus.

The traditional non-Conservative forces of reaction or radical reform can be dealt with through the usual parliamentary techniques. Their very existence is often helpful to the Conservative by supplying a challenge to be dealt with, through focusing of attention on a particular problem in need of a solution, by providing the catalytic social agent that prompts reform, or by providing the stabilizing inertia to be overcome.

The counterrevolution is unique in its non-Conservative character. Whether it is of the militant national "socialism," such as that characterized by the Nazism of German and Fascism of Italy or militant international "socialism," such as that guided by the power elite of the USSR, it requires special measures to deal with it effectively.

Perhaps the most significant feature of all counterrevolutionary forces is their direct and opposite relationship to the natural constructive development of civilization. Counterrevolution develops a doctrine and dogma that purports to answer all the questions with a finality permitting of no further consideration. The falsity of its initial premises dictates this as a matter of necessity. There can be no compromise with this closed-end system. There can be no coexistence.

One basic characteristic of the counterrevolution is its totalitarian nature. It can be recognized wherever an authoritarian regime arrogates all economic and institutional power to itself and proceeds to nullify all opposition. Der Fuhrer, El Jefe, the Enlightened One, and the Leader—messianic leadership becomes the symbol of all allegiance and authority. Because the regime is based on false premises, it becomes necessary to rule in a crisis and fear atmosphere to sustain the "mass" support. The Socialist base of the economy is unable to function successfully and thus it becomes increasingly necessary to direct the attention of the "people" abroad against foreign aggressors, imperialists, colonialists, etc., to support the constant demands for "sacrifice" in support of the "revolution," which is really the counterrevolution. Little aggressions are undertaken to assuage national pride. We witness this phenomenon at work in all Communist-dominated countries and in such nonaligned nations as Indonesia, Egypt, and Ghana.

The Conservative recognizes in international Communism the counterrevolution. The Conservative knows that this force is not to be diverted from its destructive course through attempts at accommodation and compromise. The Conservative knows that peaceful coexistence with Communism is another non-Conservative myth; perhaps the most dangerous myth of all. Just as the counterrevolutionary forces of Nazism and Fascism had to ultimately be pacified at great cost in life and treasure, and the temporary arrestation of constructive social development, so ultimately may the counterrevolutionary forces of Communism. The time may not yet be passed where Communism can be pacified without plunging the Western civilization into another civil war, but the ray of remaining hope flickers by dimly. Should we concede another position, yield just a bit more strength, and compromise one more issue, we run the risk that the last ray of hope will die. We will then have irretrievably committed ourselves to the fantastic holocaust of a nuclear war, or the loss of freedom to the counterrevolution, only to be retrieved by our children or theirs at far greater cost as the fate of the Freedom Fighters of Hungary will attest.

Individual liberty is the natural condition of man. Man either lives in a state of liberty or struggles to attain this condition. Once man has attained a state of liberty, he will not rationally and consciously surrender this state without expending all his resources even unto his life in its defense. The Conservative believes that a life without liberty is not worth living unless the energies are expended in its quest. The Conservative believes that a people are justified in waging war in quest of liberty and, further, that any war, which a people may wage, not in quest of liberty is sheer madness.

If we Americans did not believe profoundly in the eternal truth of our existence as a free people, then just the contemplation of a thermonuclear war in the defense of some other cause would mark us with insanity. To wage war to achieve "lasting peace" is just another mad dream. To wage war for national independence is fantasy and sterile of meaning. To wage a war for a standard of living or some other material purpose is to court disaster for the possession of tarnished baubles. To wage the struggle for liberty is the only cause for which man can make the ultimate sacrifice secure in the knowledge that his sacrifice was not in vain, for this is the only struggle worth waging.

There can be no compromise with Communism. There can be no neutrality in this struggle. The American people must accept unqualified responsibility for pacification of the counterrevolution or forfeit their role of leadership within the Western civilization. There is required a recognition of the fact that the struggle is joined. We must realize that it is the revolutionary development of man from a condition of servitude toward a condition of liberty that is assailed. The tactics of the counterrevolution must not be confused with the grand strategy. If we are to emerge successful from these perilous times, we must lose no more time in bringing our strength to bear in the conflict. We have lost the opportunity to deal with the menace through persuasion and parliamentary maneuver. The counterrevolution has become institutionalized and commands immense destructive power. We must face up to this reality. We must now engage this power and seek to render it impotent, to pacify it.[73]

It is not the immediate defeat of Communism that the Conservative seeks, but its pacification. The Conservative recognizes that the immediate total defeat of Communism might so convulse the world that mankind may never recover. This does not represent a compromise attitude, however, but a simple recognition of two factors. First, Communism, contained effectively and faced with ultimate defeat, likely would plunge the world into a general war as one last desperate gesture of defiance. Secondly, Communism, robbed of its militancy, rendered pacific, can be dealt with, within the existing social framework. Once militant international Socialism becomes but pacified national Socialism, it can be made to pass into the archives as but another of man's fantasy flirtations in the wake of the revolutionary advance.

Without delay, we must come to realize that this struggle between revolution and counterrevolution is not just another struggle between national states. This is not a competition between the USSR and the United States. This is a struggle being waged by a Socialist counterrevolution.

The American people are the prime target of the assailing forces. The counterrevolution has correctly identified the American people as at once the leaders and conservers of the revolutionary tradition. It is the United States and the American people who must be neutralized and rendered impotent for the counterrevolution to succeed. We must be isolated from the remainder of mankind to finally fall as a ripe plum from the tree.

It is through an understanding of the tactical and strategic necessities of the counterrevolution that we can direct our energies in leadership of the forces of freedom.

No act that we as a people perform is unrelated to the struggle. No contact that we have with the enemy of Communism is without significance. Each time our ambassador to the Soviet Union calls upon the chairman of the Council of Ministers, we deal directly with the powerful agent of the conspiracy and lend dignity to his position. Each time the ambassador of the Soviet Union is received with diplomatic courtesy by the President of United States, we acknowledge to an unsophisticated world that the United States considers him and that which he represents to be respectable. When the United States resists the Soviet Union as such, we communicate too much of mankind that we are a powerful people whose quarrel is the traditional quarrel of powerful states.

We must first communicate to the entire world through action and deed that it is the international Communist conspiracy, the counterrevolution, which we resist. Unless we clarify this point, there is little hope that we can make the rest of mankind understand our leadership. If they fail to understand, they cannot confidently follow.

Once we make clear to a waiting world the objective of our leadership, and the source of our concern, we will then be in a position to deal with the counterrevolution and all those who weaken our position by attempting to stand aside under a banner of "neutrality." There will then be no neutral ground to occupy between the poles of "East" and "West," between Moscow and Washington. The choice presented will be one of declining to participate in the only true revolutionary tradition, the final liberation of man from the tyranny of man.

We have been told repeatedly that this is an ideological struggle, that it must be waged with ideals, that superior ideology will prevail. The Conservative knows that there is but one idea which will inflame the world, and that is the idea that burns bright in the torch of liberty.

The American people will have sometimes alternately and sometimes separately flirted with the forces of the counterrevolution. To a considerable extent at home through many of the domestic policies of the New Deal, the Fair Deal and the Welfare State, we have moved in the direction of actually joining the counterrevolution. The political-economic intervention into the monetary system with the accompanying policy of inflation has worked to forge a more powerful weapon of the counterrevolution in our midst. In our foreign aid programs, we have not infrequently given assistance to the very forces that we must weaken and pacify. We have actually encouraged and strengthened the forces that are either allied with or furnished aid and comfort to the counterrevolution itself.

These courses must be recognized for what they are. If we join forces with the counterrevolution at home and encourage it abroad, we will have arrived at a position of leadership in the vanguard of the revolution to preside over the decline and passing of a civilization. Better we were to devote our talents to composing a suitable requiem.

Once we identify the counterrevolution as the force against which we wage our struggle, we are automatically in a position to take a great number of steps that are denied to us as long as we confuse the nature of the struggle with the quasi-national status of the Soviet Union.[74]

If we are to have continued contact with the Communist masters of the peoples of the Soviet Union, it might be useful to begin by distinguishing between the nature of recognition we accord the governments of the nations of the world and the regimes of Communist-dominated societies. This could involve withdrawal of diplomatic recognition with all of the inescapable implications of recognition of legitimacy and tacit approval, and substitution of a special kind of "United States Representative" to a Communist-dominated society. We could, through our withdrawal of our recognition, do much to strengthen our leadership position in resistance to the counterrevolution. This leadership has been compromised by a non-Conservative failure to deal effectively with the Communists in 1917 and again when the United States accorded recognition to the power elite of the USSR in 1933. The myth of the national status of the USSR and our relations based upon that myth has led to a whole series of compromising actions by our government.[75]

Preliminary to our reconstruction of our representation, we should reevaluate our forces that are charged with the task of dealing with the counterrevolution. There may be some utility in constituting a single agency of the government with the exclusive responsibility of framing policy to deal with the counterrevolution. The "Special United States Representative" might be agent officers of this agency and thus removed from nominal subordination to the Secretary of State.

Such a move could be dramatic evidence to all of the peoples of the world and their governments that we do not look upon the Communist regimes as similar to the legitimate governments of independent national states. We would effectively communicate our recognition that once a state is captured by a Communist power elite, it ceases to be a nation and becomes but another base and source of power for the prosecution of the Communist conspiracy, the counterrevolution.

This course involves a rejection of the policy of containment and defense in favor of offensive action. The policy of containment and defense may have been prudent during a period while we were orienting ourselves to the reality of Communism. The shattering of the non-Conservative World War II myth of Communist cooperation in rebuilding a war-torn world was severe in its impact. Time was required to heal our disoriented psyche. The time for therapy is past. We must now face up to the threat which confronts us. We will either pacify this militant force of counterrevolution or run the risk of perishing in a great fiery moment of truth.

Preliminary to the development of any grand strategy must be a careful identification of the related factors. Facts must be faced squarely, and nothing must be hidden because it seems not to fit the pattern or is uncomfortable or unsettling. One fact that must be faced by the American people that will be unsettling is the fact that "neutrality" or "neutralism" is a myth, a fantasy, and a dream. Wherever the forces of the revolution do not dominate, the forces of counterrevolution will move in to fill the void. There is no middle or neutral ground. This rather uncomfortable fact makes nonsense out of the non-Conservative position respecting the right of some governments to seek a neutral position. Power is like a great expanding gas. Wherever a vacuum exists and the gas has access, it will move into the vacuum and fill every tiny crevice. The existence of neutrality simply invites Communist penetration with the irresistible attraction of the flame to the moth.

For the United States to conspire in the development of "neutralism" is simply flirting with the possibility that counterrevolution will succeed. We cannot allow ourselves to be isolated from the remainder of mankind. We could find ourselves pressing on in the quest of liberty at the head of a nonexistent force.

We must lead first, but where our leadership is not understood, we must persuade, cajole, induce, coerce, and compel. We must extend the force of our leadership and our power beyond our borders into every corner of this earth where man dwells. Our influence must be extended into the very heart of the counterrevolution itself.

If this be imperialism, then let the counterrevolution make the most of it, for we cannot shrink from our responsibility.

One of the first things that we must do as a people is to develop an attitude of patience born of maturity. We must discard the impulsiveness and impatience of our younger days, when we were but a small frog in a very large pond. Today, we are of prodigious size, and each time we flex a digit, the entire human race is affected. We must stop asking for and expecting miracles. Let us first of all accept the fact that we are in this position for the long haul. It might be well to remember that even if we were to liberate the Russian people from the yoke of Communism this very day, the forces of counterrevolution would remain abroad in the world and would still have to be dealt with.

The American people are the best equipped to pursue this struggle and to lead the rest of Western civilization. It is in these United States that the revolution has progressed the farthest. It is here that the greatest advances have been realized toward the society in which liberty will be recognized as man's natural condition.

To cope with the counterrevolution, we have but to press on in the perfection of the revolution to which we are heir. Our task is to identify the areas where and causes why the revolution has not yet achieved the condition of liberty where each individual walks with dignity, secure in the exercise of his rights, protected by a rule of law, where equal opportunity is accorded to all, and economic justice is the basis whereby each is protected in the enjoyment of the fruits of his labor. Our role is to facilitate the natural social development of the revolution toward this condition and lead the rest of the peoples of the world in this direction. Our objective is liberty and justice for all.

The preoccupation with "world opinion" is another non-Conservative myth manifestation. It is not the accolades, the plaudits, the popular demonstrations of enthusiasm that are the reliable objectives of measure of policy. The mob is a heedless mass of humanity that is just as capable of crowning the victor with leaves of laurel on Saturday as stoning him on the following Monday. Christ was crucified with the approval of the same mob who hailed his entrance into Jerusalem. Caesar, Mussolini, Stalin, Khrushchev, and Castro have all been cheered by immense crowds. For an

American to be influenced by a popular demonstration in a foreign land is egotism but not wisdom. American leadership must rest on a firmer foundation than fickle "world opinion" whatever this may be.

The possession of superior power and the will to use that power in the judicious pursuit of the basic interests of the American people is the stuff on which sound United States policy is based. The great source of our power is the very fact that we are identified with and lead the revolution tradition. This aligns us with the full force of man's natural development. When all our immense strength and energy is applied to the facilitation of the advancement of the revolution, our strength embraces all of the strength of those millions who struggle for liberty.

The leader must always be wise in his restraint but never timid. Timidity is not characteristic of leadership, nor is it a characteristic of a people who would live free. If need be, we must have the courage to stand alone. If we communicate to the world that we will stand alone in our strength, firm in the right, we will never find our side deserted. It is when we present to the world a picture of vacillation, compromise, timidity, and solicitous regard for the irrational and irresponsible behavior of others that many who would otherwise confidently follow, falter and turn aside.

Harsh as the fact may seem to the squeamish, the intensification of the internal problems of the Communist-dominated societies may be one of the most fruitful and least hazardous of all the avenues open. It is a nice sentimental expression of charity to say; in effect, we disdain to use food as a weapon, but this may be just another way of saying that we prefer the clean, fiery extinction of a nuclear war to the positive waging of the struggle against the counterrevolution. If we are to succeed in pacifying international Communism so that it can be dealt with without resort to war, we should not allow sentimentality to obscure the fact that institutionalized Communism has demonstrated certain basic weaknesses, and an inability to develop a productive agriculture is one of the most notable. If we can compound and exploit this weakness through withholding assistance or bargaining hard for any assistance rendered, the effect might be startling.

The Conservative recognizes in the great economic power of the United States a force that needs but to be liberated, turned loose to extend the constructive influence of the American people and their leadership throughout the world. The economic power of the American people and their allies dwarfs all of the power at the command of the counterrevolution. The Conservative would seek to direct this power toward the further prosecuting of the revolution and thus rob the counterrevolution of opportunities for penetration and extension.

To achieve this liberation, the Conservative would say to the American citizen, "Go forth, risk, undertake promising enterprises, extend your influence throughout the remotest areas of this earth. Go abroad and build, develop, trade, and produce abundance. Bring the blessings of abundance to the peoples of the world so that they may achieve a condition of individual liberty free from dependence on the bounty of other men. Go abroad into foreign lands and enter into productive and constructive relationships with the peoples of those lands. Teach them by example through these relationships that it is man's natural condition to live free. Let them see in you and your works the dynamism and productiveness of a free society. Let the peoples of the world see in you the characteristics of dignity, self-confidence, and responsibility, which are the attributes of free citizens in a free society."

The Conservative would say to these tens of thousands of free Americans who ventured far from the comfort of their homes, "Go with the knowledge that your fellow citizens and their government, your government, approves of what you do. It, your government, remains your servant, and will provide you with the same protection which is accorded to all citizens."

The Conservative would caution the citizens who venture abroad that they must not expect their government to do more for them than is done for the millions of their fellow citizens, but they could remain confident that their interests would not be the subject of discrimination. The citizen doing business in a foreign land would be assured that his government was using its power to bring into existence or improve the existing environment, where enterprise can be profitably pursued by individuals under a system of law.

The Conservative knows that the world must not be allowed to drift while the forces of counterrevolution are abroad. The United States cannot allow itself to be isolated from mankind through misguided concern for the sensibilities of the vain and pompous. The struggle is much too real to allow for such indulgence. The proud assertion of national independence by a social group which is neither national nor independent, could be accorded the status of comic opera at some other less perilous time, but now to indulge such assertions could prove tragic. To gear the policies of the United States to the often irrational and frequently irresponsible expressions of these "almost nations" is sheer folly. To take pride in the fact of being able to "line up" a majority of votes from these sources in support of some watered-down tasteless resolution in the UN General Assembly is not leadership. The leader is the captive of the led.

The epithets of "Yankee imperialism" must not dissuade us from our chartered course. "Dollar diplomacy" is not to be eschewed. The Conservative is not to be intimidated from venturing forth by blandishments about capitalistic neocolonialism. These are recognized as counterrevolutionary dirty words. When they are applied by the forces of Communism, heart should be taken for there has been some degree of success.

Coincident with this impulse of private economic activity by American citizens throughout the world should come the communication from the United States government to the governments of foreign lands: "If you choose to stand aside and not to join us in this struggle, then you cannot expect us to expend our treasure to subsidize and assist you." The Conservative would let the peoples of the world know that the United States is generous to its friends, correct with its nonfriendly neighbors, and unremitting in the pursuit of its enemies. Neutralism would be actively discouraged and never rewarded. Nothing less is in accord with the basic interests of the American people.

A nation, a power, a civilization either develops or declines. It grows and expands or it contracts. The perpetuation of static relationships is not possible. If the United States does not grow more powerful, it will be eclipsed, and probably absorbed by a greater power. This very eventuality is currently being forecast by many who see so much for the future of European unity. The possibility that this may prove ultimately to be an accurate forecast need not influence the United States' immediate course, for in any event, it is our interest that Europe come together and wax powerful and strong.

The main objective in the waging of economic warfare against the forces of Communism is to bring about a general weakening of the internal Communist structure. The unification of the Western European market promises to bring into existence an economic force, which properly exploited, could draw the satellites of Eastern Europe as a magnet. The West European nations have traditional relationships with East European peoples. These can and should be exploited. The result could substantially weaken the prevailing dependent economic ties with the USSR. The consequence could be the actual conversion of the new satellite regimes into national socialistic governments. In this event, a significant step would be taken in the pacification of militant international socialism.

The United States could take the initiative in creating an allied economic warfare planning group, which would work out strategic and tactical plans to deal with the problems of direct economic pressure on the forces of Communism. Once the United States has taken the initiative and pressed toward the creation of a worldwide free trade area and has extended economic integration of economic interest through the participation of American interests in enterprises throughout the world, the nations of the world would see it in their interest to follow our lead.

When it is recognized that the extension of American economic interests is the cornerstone of our leadership, then it follows that the international security of commerce and property becomes of substantial concern. Free access to the markets of the world is a prerequisite to dynamic international commercial development. This means uninterruptable access.

The sea lanes cannot be allowed to be shut off by any power in an act hostile to ours or allied interests. This has particular application to the Suez and Panama Canals. We might just as well be candid about the matter. Freedom of the seas and access to all the world waterways is a fundamental requirement to the security interest of the American people. We cannot permit a Nasser in Egypt or any hostile force in the Caribbean to interrupt our passage through any waterway.

Passageways to commerce are vital, but they are not the anchor points of interest throughout the more remote areas of the world. The United States has a direct interest in Hong Kong, Singapore, Gibraltar, Okinawa, etc. These are anchor points of influence. Their loss would only compound the difficulties of exercising influence in the adjacent areas.

In approaching the problem of the counterrevolution presented by militant international socialism or communism, there is an election to be made. We can join it; we can seek to quarantine it, contain it, and isolate it, or we can actively oppose them. Like Hamlet, "to be or not to be" is our question. The Conservative has chosen to be and "actively take up arms against the sea of troubles and by so opposing, end them."

Once the decision is made to oppose actively, we are presented with the problem of the military commander who is given a mission to perform with the limited resources available.

First, the commander must construct an estimate of the situation incorporating an identification of the enemy and his capabilities, the possible and probably courses of action that the enemy is likely to pursue, the avenues open to the commander in the pursuit of his mission. Finally, certain promising courses will be selected and plans are drawn. When the forces are committed, the commander will subject the developing situation to continuing review, remaining always flexible and adaptable to accommodate his plans and action to the changing situation.

One of the most critical parts of the commander's estimate is his intelligence estimate, the estimate of the enemy. This involves knowing the enemy and requires reliance upon information supplied by many sources and evaluated by sophisticated and reliable analysts. The Conservative recognizes that the counterrevolution must be studied, learned about, and understood. It is only from this position of knowledge that promising action can be initiated.

The outline of the particular military posture that is dictated lies beyond the scope of these considerations. The private citizens do not have the technical data available upon which to base judgments with respect to weapons selection or the mode of their employment. The particular military posture decisions can prudently be left to the experts and the professionals. It is our role, however, to instruct our civilian representatives as to the particular strategic considerations that lie within our knowledge.

It lies entirely within our field of judgment as citizens to so instruct our representatives, that we wish to assume the initiative in dealing with the forces of the counterrevolution. We must say to those who are accountable to us, proceed to pacify this force of reaction, this militant international Socialism, render it impotent.

When we assume the initiative and begin the pacification of Communism, we must anticipate great tensions to develop within the empire now controlled by the counterrevolution. United States military strength will have to remain sufficiently strong throughout this period to effectively discourage any adventures outside the empire to relieve this internal pressure. The regular establishment must become in effect the reserve; and the reserves, the regulars. What is meant by this is that the regular military forces must be retained intact and ready for action in the event of general nuclear engagement with the main forces of the counterrevolution, the Red Army of the USSR. We cannot permit the systems that are designed to deliver nuclear weapons to be dissipated in limited encounters with the secondary forces of the conspiracy. If the regular forces are committed to such operations, the strategic deterrent could be substantially compromised and general vulnerability increased.

There is required a general recognition of the role of the National Guard and the Reserve Forces in active support of United States interests short of general war. Much more attention must be directed to these forces. The units should be equipped with the most advanced tactical weapons and receive periodic and regular training in the use of these weapons. The casual stop and go manner of reserve administration should be discontinued without delay. Mobilization and demobilization should be worked out on a routine basis, and care should be taken that the weight of service should be equitably distributed among all citizens. This would go a long way toward eliminating the discriminating features of the Selective Service System. Some sort of universal military training seems to be a promising solution where none would be favored by reason of occupation, family condition, or otherwise in escaping his responsibilities as a citizen.

Above all, we must instruct our representatives that we wish them to become thoroughly familiar with the nature of the counterrevolution and to learn what is required to cope with the problems "presented." We must tell those who are responsible that we seek the pacification of international

Communism and not coexistence with it. The mission is thus identified; there but remains to be developed a grand strategy, a design, a national plan of action, and then to get on with the job.

Any development of a "grand design" should accommodate several important considerations. The first and most significant of which might be stated as flexibility.

Flexibility has been a crucial problem to military planners for thousands of years. The early Greeks had developed a most powerful military formation called the Phalanx. This was an infantry formation of sixteen columns deep, armed with swords and pikes. This formation was indeed formidable when backed up by light cavalry. That this formation was too inflexible to deal with the Roman legion accounts at least partially for the conquest of Greece by Rome. History records countless walled cities of Europe reduced through the offensive tactics of the Great Khan. Prior to World War II, General de Gaulle had written a professional evaluation of the use of light armored forces in the art of penetration and exploitation of breakthroughs. Hitler built Panzer units and developed the art of "blitzkrieg." The French built the Maginot Line. Later, Hitler ignored some of his own advisors and failed to develop a strategic bomber force. He relied on "Festung Europa" and the fortifications of the "Atlantic Wall" to shield his empire from allied assault. On June 6, 1944, all of Der Fuhrer's illusions were shattered on the beaches of Normandy.

There is always the danger that military postures may become static and inflexible.

Three characteristic afflictions of the American political thinking processes must go. Our clarity of purpose is only clouded through myth-think, wish-think, and jabberwocky. We must actively dissipate our illusions and recognize the world for what it is and not cling to dreams of what we would like it to be. Once we have accomplished this, we must begin to communicate to our representatives in meaningful terms and demand that they respond no less meaningfully.

We must do our homework and study the nature of the contest in which we are engaged. This study will include an inquiry into the places, ways, and whys, which our efforts have miscarried in the past. It is mandatory, however, that our investigations are not vengeful. We need light and not heat. Tactical errors have been made, but it is far more likely that this can be attributed to a propensity for illusion rather than disposition toward treason.

Myth and illusion have been a characteristic of our thinking concerning the counterrevolution since Wilson's Ambassador to Moscow failed to comprehend the Bolshevik seizure of power. The myths have tended to discount fact and to ground belief on what the counterrevolutionists represented themselves to be. Our historic approach to "Uncle Joe" Stalin, the Lincoln Brigade, and the Spanish Civil War, the entire participation of the USSR in World War II, the Chinese "agrarian reformers," the liberal revolution led by Castro in Cuba, and in the years of 1961–1962, coexistence and the need to support Khrushchev against his militant communist opposition, all are characteristic.

The web of fantasy has been woven into the very fabric of our policy with respect to the counterrevolution wherever that policy is to be found. The Roosevelt policy of "four-power cooperation," the Truman policy of "containment," and the Eisenhower-Dulles policy of "liberation" all had fatal flaws. Massive retaliation has some of the same flaws of inflexibility, as does the Kennedy concept of "balance of terror" and conventional forces to fight conventional limited wars. On the one hand, we stand squarely facing our adversary with hand poised inches from the button that will plunge the entire world into war. Our hope is that the aggressor will be rational and thus restrain any dangerous impulses. On the other hand, we advertise our readiness to engage in limited wars for limited prizes. The aggressor is encouraged to believe that he can undertake adventures that can be controlled. Each approach is filled with danger, and neither addresses itself to the real problem, that of the ultimate pacification of the counterrevolution.

Our task is not simply to dissuade the Communist from initiating general military action or to do so in limited areas with conventional forces. Our task is to deprive international communism of its militancy and its aggressive character and to advance the condition of liberty. It is in these terms that we must talk to those who represent us. This is meaningful discourse.

If those who represent us are to act with boldness, with daring, then they must have our assurance that they will not be penalized for reasonable failures. We must recognize that the pacification of the counterrevolution will entail the assumption of calculated risks. Each risk must be understood to carry with it the possibility of failure. Every bold, imaginative undertaking cannot be expected to be crowned with unqualified success. Our objective is pacification while avoiding the general engagement of the strategic forces. To achieve this objective, our tacticians and strategists must be creative, innovative, and imaginative.

Conservative criticism of "Cold War" policy and action will be one that recognizes the need for innovation and imagination. The inherent risk of failure in bold enterprises will be accepted. U-2 incidents are to be expected. The criticism of the "Cuban invasion" is based upon the timidity and vacillation in the execution and not the initiative which set the enterprise in motion. Criticism of the Berlin matter is not related to the initiative that advanced proposals to liquidate the exposed American position but to the lack of imagination and weakness that did not anticipate and acquiesced in the building of the "Wall." The Conservative will not be diverted by some attempts by a peripatetic and loquacious President to elevate "talk, talk, talk" to a position of prestige above wisdom and firm action in pursuit of American interests. When China is ultimately convulsed as a Hungary, criticism will likely be appropriately directed at a confused China and Asia policy that did not comprehend, anticipate, and thus did not prepare. The indications are clear.

As we pursue our investigations into the nature of the counterrevolution, the reality of its power, and its penetration into our society, let us exercise an abundance of caution lest we do violence to the very traditions that we seek to conserve. Just as it was without justice to arbitrarily deprive persons of Japanese ancestry of their liberty and property without regard to their constitutional rights, it is wrong to capriciously identify or infer association with the counterrevolution.

In the pursuit of our investigations, we must guard against sowing the seeds of discord and fabricating the dark clouds of suspicion. This does not mean that we should be less firm and positive in our activities to expose the counterrevolution. It does mean that we dare not compromise civil liberties in the process.

Let the full weight of our indictment be leveled against those who would silence inquiry. It is the politician who seeks to avoid the public consequences for his lack of judgment through silencing inquiry under the guise of the "public interest" who deserves our contempt. Such efforts to prevent disclosure to the public are a disservice to the Republic, and the politician must be held accountable.

There remains one additional point to be considered and that is the magnitude of our resources that are committed to the matter of defense. As this increases, there is raised the possibility that we may find our liberty eroded away under the weight of the burden. There is the ever-present possibility that we could develop such intense vested interests in the engines and industries of war that much of our essential flexibility could be lost. There is even the possibility that this could happen related to a specific weapons system. This is an area that requires constant attention if we are not to lose that which we seek to conserve.

Never must we become so fascinated by one aspect of the problem that we are in danger of losing our perspective. It is the advancement of the revolution that is the objective, and the counterrevolution must be pacified because it threatens the orderly and constructive advance.

XII
THE PART ASSIGNED TO US

Now is the time to speak of many things. The time for talk then passes, and the time arrives when we must decide whether to "fish or cut bait," whether to stand at the wall, towel in hand, and bewail at the passing of liberty or step forth and take part in the "action and passions" of our time. The choice is to participate or to suffer the future to be the product of the actions of others. The authentic Conservative has no election. He can only decline to participate at the risk of becoming a social parasite, thereby forfeiting his essential Conservative character. The Conservative knows that the culture, the forms, the heritage of liberty must be possessed, acted upon, synthesized, and passed on to eager young hands as current, viable aspects of the civilizing process, lest man's development cease and the age of darkness descend upon the earth.

We could go on considering one aspect after another of our relationships with our fellow man. I could seek to relate each particular issue raised to the Conservative position as I conceive it, and I could hope that this would serve to encourage each of us to consider and reconsider his own attitudes. The number of issues that could engage our attention would be as long and as varied as the relations of man. The tedium of such a presentation would be immense. I would be presuming on my reader's patience far more than would be my right. I have selected the issues that I have discussed here because I think they present an opportunity of exposing the relationship of the Conservative position to representative issues that engage our attention in our time. I have stated what I have stated here because this is the way I look upon these things. I have tried to be consistent in relating my understanding of the Conservative position to the issues, in the hope that this would yield a reliable guide to action, which would promise to lead toward the realization of the Conservative society, where individual liberty would be universally recognized as the natural condition of man.

Many readers might wonder at this point why I have chosen not to discuss such important issues as freedom of inquiry, expression, and assembly. What of "freedom of the press" and censorship? What of "freedom of religion" and the right to worship or not as one sees fit? What would the Conservative have to say with respect to "academic freedom" and the qualification of teachers? I am not seeking to avoid these matters, nor do I suggest that they do not present very difficult and profound questions, when controversy surrounds their exercise. I would simply say this in illustration of the application of the Conservative position. In each case, the Conservative would ask the preliminary question: "Freedom for what?" The answer to this crucial question should lead to reliable Conservative action. If academic freedom means to condition the minds of the young with myth and idolatry, then this is a non-Conservative dogma and is to be resisted. The Conservative concept of "academic freedom" involves the freedom to pursue and to seek the truth. It does not involve the licensing of some citizens to seek to influence the immature minds of our children with closed-end concepts, with "-isms," with prejudicial ideas, and error.

Before we begin to discuss some promising courses of Conservative action, I would draw the reader's attention to one or two points which seem of particular importance to me. First of all, I would point out that I have not used the term *conservatism*. This has been intentional and with specific purpose. I do not conceive of the Conservative position of embracing a dogma or doctrine, a particular philosophy, or a set of logically related principles. The reason why the Conservative position is unrelated to any "-ism" or "-ology" is just because of the understanding that such do embrace doctrine, dogma, and a mythology. The Conservative position embraces an attitude toward the matter of living and does not comprehend a set of principles to be enshrined as an idol. The Conservative recognizes in the non-Conservative a disposition to enshrine ideas, concepts, philosophies, and even institutions and then to worship at the shrines. For the Conservative, there is but one God, the true God, and all other gods are but graven images and false. Liberalism, Socialism, Communism, Fascism, individualism, nationalism, Americanism, science, etc., are all false gods, which are destined to fail the faithful. The Conservative recognizes in all of the works of man, but tools to be employed by each in accordance with his needs in the pursuit of his unique individual development.

Much confusion with respect to the Conservative position disappears when we understand that the terms *freedom* and *liberty* are not just two terms describing the same thing. The Conservative understands *freedom* as the natural, the essential condition of man. It is the condition of each human being as he stands in direct relation to God. To the Christian, this means that man was made free through Christ, when God made man whole through reconciling to God. Freedom involves man's conceptual capacity, his faculty of choice, and delayed response to stimuli. It is this very profound and radical freedom of man, which accounts for his apparent perverseness or unpredictability. *Liberty* is essentially corporeal. It is the state of the absence of coercive restraint. It involves all of the social and political freedoms that are characteristic of modern democratic societies. It is a relative concept and a condition of social significance, where man has recognized the need to provide a social condition that corresponds to the essential freedom of man's nature.

We see that the Conservative position involves something far different from an ideological basis purporting to underlie the Conservative position. The Conservative worships no graven images of wood, stone, parchment, or apparatus. It is not a faith in any man, institution, or system. The Conservative faith is alone in God. Being a Conservative is to have an attitude toward living. The Conservative acts are the glue that holds the works of man together in a way that each individual will be afforded the social freedom to pursue his own individual destiny. In this sense, the fact of being a Conservative comprehends far more than being a Democrat or Republican but is not inconsistent with either party affiliation. Each individual Conservative remains free to pursue his own development and to achieve his own peace, and yet there remains a characteristic and constant attitude toward life, which is detectible.

This Conservative attitude is reflected in the shining eyes of the tourist who stands before the Lincoln Memorial in our nation's capital. This attitude is manifested in the act of the hunter, breaking the match with which he has just ignited his cigarette. We see it in the Cub Scout "Den Mother" and the "Scout Master," who give so much of themselves that young people will grow straight and tall. The "old soldier" who stands proud as the flag goes by shows an attachment to his heritage, which is characteristic of the Conservative. It is the attitude of one who knows that he walks this way but one time and is determined that he will give more than he receives so that his children and their children and theirs after them will find the resources and the environment in which they too may enjoy their liberty and exercise their unalienable rights.

The Conservative walks among the giant Sequoias and thanks God for the pure joy that is his on this day. He looks on the sunlight streaming down from the heavens, filtered by the rich green lacy branches, to fall gently on the soft carpet of the forest floor, and he reflects that he now stands in a great natural cathedral that had its birth three thousand years and more than seven hundred generations before him. He walks with care lest he destroy the new growth or does injury to the old that this source of man's shelter and joy will not perish at his hand. He reaches out and removes a parasite or uproots sucker growth that this enduring form will be stronger, more vital, and better able to shelter those who walk after him. His profound wish is that the world he leaves behind, which has given him so much, will be even more fruitful by reason of his having walked this way.

The Conservative looks upon man as a natural creature, subject to the demands of natural appetites, with a unique capacity of sublimating or satisfying those appetites as he chooses. This freedom to deny or gratify his appetitive nature sets man apart from all other creatures and accounts for his apparent perversity. The Conservative recognizes, in this freedom aspect of man's nature, that element that will never permit reliable predictability. This understanding does not, however, discourage the Conservative in his pursuit of knowledge. He accepts as fact that there exist certain limits to his potential for understanding. Certain things that will always remain obscure, and man's freedom is perhaps one of the most obscure. The Conservative accepts science and its method as a useful tool in describing and interpreting historical evidence and makes full use of projections grounded in these interpretations but remains aware of man's natural freedom and his faculty of choice and thus leaves the door wide open for the anticipated unexpected. The Conservative is never paralyzed into inaction by reason of this limited knowledge. He lives responsibly, prudently, and speculatively, probing and searching, always keeping the end open for constructive development.

Because man is a free creature endowed with the faculty of choice and thereby can deny or gratify his appetites as he sees fit, man has achieved a certain mastery over his physical environment. This mastery has permitted man to multiply and compelled him to congregate and to compete. Thus, it is in the very act of living as a human being that man experiences all those tensions that are characteristic of his relationships with his environment and his fellow man. These tensions are the force, which at once hold society together, and at the same time, permit each individual to stand apart and develop his own unique capabilities, his personality. As individuals are born, grow to maturity, live active and productive lives, and then pass from the mortal scene, relationships among men constantly change. Existing tensions constantly adjust to the shifting relationships, and it is in these constantly changing relationships and resolution of the adjusting tensions that Conservative constructive development proceeds. Man has the capacity of frustrating this resolution through the exercise of his faculty of choice. When static relationships are introduced, the resolution is inhibited and forces build that will ultimately break loose with convulsive consequences. Conservative competition becomes conflict, strife, and ware. Conservative peace is the condition characteristic of man's relationships where an equilibrium is maintained among the competing forces such that the tension resolution proceeds constantly and constructively.

The Conservative knows that poverty, ignorance, disease, and decadence are not the products of industrialization, capitalism, or communism. Pestilence, famine, man's inhumanity to man are as old as the age of man. Peace, as an absence of conflict among men, is to be realized in another day when man has made peace first with God. It is not to be realized through contracts, institutions, or balances of forces and terror. The best that can be hoped for is that we will achieve a modest peace in our time. This is the Conservative objective. This is a worthy objective, however, only if we use the time to seek more intelligent relationships among men where their persisting conflicts can be resolved in an atmosphere of order and law. In the meantime, the Conservative stands alert and keeps his powder dry.

The objectives are limited, but they are real. They are those which are without the color of myth, fantasy, or dream. They are of this world and are modest, humble, prudent, and humane. The course does not permit that one man be committed to slavery, that two might live free. The greater good to the greater number can never mean one inalienable right can be sacrificed to the welfare of the many.

The Conservative asks not, "What can my government do for me?" Nor does he ask, "What can I do for my government?" The Conservative asks, "What can I do for my country, my fellow citizen, my fellow man?" Once he asks these questions, he looks not elsewhere for the answer but within himself. He seeks the answer within his own knowledge of his capabilities, his potentials, and his relationship to the environment in which he lives. He knows that, as a free man, his first responsibility is to himself and his own development and to facilitate the development of those dependent upon him. His service is not to be performed as some kind of penance in some far-off land. His service is to his fellow man within the community within which he lives. It is performed through the very act of living as a responsible, productive individual, conscious that the fact of living within the society of his fellow citizens entails certain obligations and duties to be performed. The Conservative recognizes these obligations and duties as the privileges of a free man.[76]

XIII
WHERE DO WE GO FROM HERE?

The question has often been asked of me, "What can we do to make our position felt?" How can we Conservatives become politically effective? How can we have a popular appeal to the millions of voters who just want more and more assistance from the Treasury? To these questions, I have answered that we (the Conservatives) are already far more effective than you realize. To be sure, we have not had the spectacular success of electing to the highest office in the land, a Conservative, who is articulate in the communication of his beliefs. True enough, we have not had the ego-pleasing pleasure of having the nation's press come forth to generally champion our position. But these apparent failures should be viewed in perspective.

First of all, we should remember that the president is elected by popular vote. Without being the least bit uncomplimentary to the individual voters who comprise the electorate, this is a very ineffective method of selecting the president. The pure eyewash and baloney that is peddled to the American voters during the presidential campaigns should be evident to all. Campaign promises are simply attempts to buy votes from voters with hot air, who are emotional enough to respond to such pie-in-the-sky proposals. The secret, and it is a very open one, to winning a presidential election is to align yourself with the political machines of the country, have enough physical and intellectual charm that the propagandists can superimpose an attractive mythical image, and then promise everyone something and call vaguely and imprecisely for sacrifice so that no one will feel that he really means me.

As far as journalistic coverage and sympathy is concerned, we should not expect too much from the nation's press. Many newspapermen are just not equipped psychologically to comprehend the Conservative position. These writers are accustomed to meeting "deadlines," and they constantly are impatient with the individual who fails to solve the problem by the time the writer must file his copy. Our newspapers are so operated that it is the spectacular, the startling, and the momentous that engages the attention of the newspaperman. He learns to expect something new and a new approach to the problem, and he is just never drawn to the artful practitioner who carefully, doggedly, and reliably brings about a working arrangement, which serves to facilitate constructive development toward an improved situation, leaving the end open for another artful practitioner to come along tomorrow in another environment and facilitate further constructive development.

The newspaperman is mesmerized by the activity of idealists and often fails to distinguish activity from action and ideals from ideas. There is a sort of self-conscious recognition of this inadequacy in the nation's press displayed in the manner in which they refer to the Conservative as "arch," "ultra," "reactionary," "right wing," or some other uncomplimentary term. There seems to be just a little display of the tendency to damn that which you cannot have. Many pseudo-intellectuals belonging to what the Duke of Wellington called "the scribbling set" tend to identify themselves with the potential "power elite" of the non-Conservative forces. Their objectivity becomes confused with illusions and dreams of power.

The Conservative is not intimidated by the attachment of the emotionally charged adjectives employed by the non-Conservative. He recognizes that the non-Conservative is frustrated by reason and truth when he attempts to assail the Conservative position. The Conservative recognizes in such terms as *arch, ultra, reactionary, right wing, far right*, etc. this non-Conservative attempt at diversion and substitution of appeal to emotion. Armed with this understanding, the Conservative can confidently proclaim his position in the knowledge that he stands where such men as Burke, Washington, Lincoln, Theodore Roosevelt, and Churchill have stood before him.

The Conservative should not feel ineffective because he has not had the satisfying appearance of the vindication of his position by capturing the highest office of the land or obtaining the approval of the press.

Neither of these things is essential, and their desirability is even debatable. The Conservative can but look about him and see that the society in which he lives has achieved the highest state of freedom for all that has ever been achieved. Opportunity is more widely accessible to each individual than has been achieved anywhere else in man's history. Of course, liberty is not a condition with equal meaning to all within our society, but this remains an open-ended system, and we are moving in that direction. These very facts are the vindication of the Conservative position.

Some of my friends have said to me almost wistfully I wish all of the Conservatives could get together. What they had in mind was some kind of Conservative organization to concentrate the Conservative influence in politics. They even suggest the formation of a Conservative political party to rival the Democrats and Republicans. In answer to this, I have reminded my friends that being a Conservative is much more than being a Democrat or Republican. Being a Conservative embraces our way of life. To attempt to construct a political institution, a set of principles, a common position, and a program that could comprehend all of the attitudes of Conservatives at one time would tend to rob the Conservative attitude of each individual of the dynamism, which is inherent in the very individual relationship. To institutionalize the Conservative position into a "Conservative party" espousing "conservatism" would subject this force to the same destructive influences that characterize all institutions, "-isms," and ideologies.

Following this observation, the further question is invariably posed: "If we shouldn't organize and politic, what should we do?" At this point, I generally must remind my friends that I did not suggest that we should not organize. What I suggested was that we should not institutionalize. I must confess that the distinction is difficult to see, but I shall try to explain what I mean. What I am saying is that there should not be created an institutional structure where there would develop a hierarchical power elite, vested interests, and institutional set of principles and objectives. We Conservatives must always guard against the reality of power in the knowledge that its nature is corruptive of men and corrosive of principle.

Our organizations should be local in character, with nothing more than coordinated liaison among them. What I would propose is some sort of a local alliance of fellow individual Conservatives, for the purpose of dealing with local issues and problems. These Conservative Alliance Groups would occupy themselves with such problems of the public schools, administration of justice in the local courts, civic improvements, children's affairs, and all of the thousands of other matters that engage the attention of the citizen in the community. Great opportunities are presented to establish liaison with Conservatives of all regions of the nation and all nations of the world. The very essence of the Conservative position encourages this. The intranational and international intercourse among Conservatives could be expected to magnify effective action through increased knowledge and understanding.

Conservatives should bear in mind that the non-Conservative had directed his attention and energies to a considerable degree away from the local community. This has left a power vacuum that is but waiting to be filled. I would suggest that we concentrate on the task of filling the lowest elective posts with bright, articulate, personable Conservatives. Devote our attention to city councils, boards of supervisors, school boards, state legislatures, and congress. Here are the areas where the Conservative can hope to make the most startling immediate impressions.

Men of responsibility and stature should engage themselves in the problems of local government. The Conservative must not be seduced by the glamour of the Potomac or even the State Capitol and allow the local affairs to drift aimlessly. It is worse than idle for the Conservative to wring his hands over the tendency for the people to look to Washington for the solution of their pesky problems and, at the same time, fail to sustain those local forms that can offer the only effective alternative. The Conservative cannot, in clear conscience, deplore and decry the trend toward federal tax financing of the local school and at the same time allow the local school to fall into disrepair and to flounder without guidance. It is not responsible to try to resist the tendency to shift all state burdens to Washington and, at the same time, pay little attention to the representative in the State Capitol.

The party label under which the candidate runs is of little significance. The principal concern is whether the candidate is a Conservative or a non-Conservative. If he is a Conservative, we must support him or her with our money, our time, and our vote. I would not suggest that a Conservative change his party association, unless he found that it was absolutely impossible to give expression to his views within his own party. The energies of the Conservative should be devoted toward influencing the selection of the most nearly Conservative candidate from his own party and, then in the general election, freely cross party lines to elect the most nearly Conservative. By way of influencing the incumbent, we might let it be known that any incumbent who followed a non-Conservative line in office would be voted out of office at the next election, even though the replacement was of the same political complexion regardless of party affiliation.

We Conservatives should orient our political activities toward the advancement of the interests of Conservatives and the influencing of the non-Conservatives toward a conservative position. No aspect of government, society, or relations among men should escape our attention. No service or duty should be too lacking of prestige and significance for us to perform.

I would suggest to those Conservatives who feel that they wish to come together in the company with others of like persuasion that they constitute themselves into an alliance with their neighbors. I would conceive of this gathering as a sort of Conservative town meeting where local problems could be thrashed out and promising approaches to problems could be proposed. These town meetings could be educational in the sense that all could contribute something of himself and his own ideas of what it means to live as a Conservative. The meaning, the strategy, and the tactics of the counterrevolution would be a fruitful subject of study. I would suggest, however, that a similar amount of attention be given to the true revolutionary tradition lest we become preoccupied with what we must resist and lose sight of what we must conserve and advance. These town meetings of a sort could provide an opportunity for much useful exchange of information and suggestions of how each individual Conservative can use his position of influence in society to guide social development along constructive lines of development.

As I see it, the Conservative should avoid attempting to fight collectively for or against anything. Let this be the tactics of the non-Conservative. The non-Conservative must marshal great collective forces to even achieve a ripple in the stream because he moves in a path counter to natural development. The Conservative has all of the force of constructive social evolution working for him. When the Conservative identifies with the true course of civilization, he immediately aligns himself with the power of all who have walked before and stands atop their shoulders and is fortified by their wisdom. Each Conservative, working as a free individual can bring his influence to bear in a thousand ways. As a free agent, he can make his position felt and reflected in the actions of every association that he has with his fellow man.

If the Conservative is a member of an industrial union, he can influence the course of those policies or, if not, just the thinking of the membership. This same man might be associated with the Boy Scouts, a hunting club, a fraternal organization, and a church group. In the process of just living a Conservative life among his fellow men, he has hundreds of opportunities to bring his influence to bear. The lawyer has opportunities through a multitude of associations and has great opportunities for service, not the least of which is the local legal assistance offices. The physician has the opportunity to serve his fellow citizens through the donation of his professional services periodically to those who are unable to afford the fee. The teacher can influence the reading habits of her students such that they derive their knowledge of the source of Western civilization from source documents and not biased colorless distillations. The teacher can influence the study of history such that the Declaration of Independence, the Constitution, and the writings of Washington, Adams, Madison, Monroe, Jefferson, and Lincoln are included. These are but a few examples of the opportunities presented to us all. Let us take our lessons from the art of judo and make full use of the weight of those with whom we grapple to influence the course of their fall.

Each of us can draw our strength from the knowledge that ours is the position that is in accord with the natural condition of man. We can proudly proclaim to the world that we live a Conservative life. We can express Conservative attitudes with consistency and need never apologize for the means employed and hasten to explain that tomorrow will see the justification. We Conservatives have at our disposal, all of the momentum of man's development. This is our force. This is our strength. We need not build great institutions for the institutions are built. We need not expend our energies in forming great collective concentrations of power, for the collectives are built. We Conservatives but need to achieve greater and greater positions of influence in the institutions and organizations already there. Each Conservative should recognize that the tendency of the many to let slide and to say, "Let George do it," to look to their government for assistance and guidance is the Conservative opportunity and the weakness of the non-Conservative. Each Conservative should recognize this tendency as an opportunity to step forward and say, "My name is George and I will do it. Choose me as your representative." What is needed is a general recognition among Conservatives that the opportunities for leadership are at hand, and all that is required is for each to stand up, step forth, and be counted.

Endnotes

1. "If the end must be used to condone the means, then there is something in the end itself, in its reality, which is not worthy. That which really blesses the end, which justifies the efforts and sacrifices for it, is the means: their constant perfection, humanness, increasing freedom." Milovan Djilas, *The New Class: An Analysis of the Communist System*, (N.Y. Praeger, 1957), p. 162.
2. The reference is to the concept of the external will conceived by Rousseau as being sovereign. This lies at the base of the modern secular religion with its implicit faith in systems of ideas. The concept is most frequently encountered today in expressions of the "national interest" comprehended or not. For the "national interest" or "general will" to become a subjective reality, it must become an expression of "the people." If "the people" do not spontaneously express it, they must be made to express it. Within this context it is the role of the "legislator" or modern "executive" to identify the "truth" or national interest, endorse that "national interest," and then employ all persuasive and coercive tools of the state to make "the people" identify with this "truth."
3. "Liberty of thought is in itself good, but it gives an opening to false liberty. Now by Liberalism I mean false liberty of thought, upon matters in which, from the constitution of the human mind, thought cannot be brought to any successful issue . . ." Cardinal John Henry Newman, Appendix on *Liberalism to Apologia Pro Vita Sua*, 1865, N.Y. and London 1892 edition, p. 285–297.
4. Sir Richard F. Burton about 1880 used the term as follows: "The Rule of Law emancipates man; and its exceptions are the gaps left by ignorance."
5. *Black's Law Dictionary, Third Edition*, defines Constitution as "the organic and fundamental law of a nation or state, which may be written or unwritten, establishing the character and conception of government, laying the basic principles to which its internal life is to be conformed, organizing the government and regulating, disturbing, and limiting the function of its departments, and prescribing the extent and manner of the exercise of sovereign powers. A charter of government deriving its whole authority from the governed."

6. "The view that inspired our Constitution... has much in common with that of Burke." Irving Babbitt, *Democracy and Leadership*, Boston, Houghton, Mifflin, 1924, pp. 243–237.
7. "Necessity is the plea for every infringement of human freedom. It is the arguments of tyrants; it is the creed of slaves." William Pitt.
8. Burke, "Reflections on the Revolution in France" (1790), *Works*, Vol. II, p. 368.
9. "The individual is foolish; the multitude, for the moment, is foolish when they act without deliberation; but the species is wise, and, when time is given to it, as a species it always acts right." Burke's *Works*, Vol. VII, Bohn's edition, London, 1861, p. 146f (Reform of Representation in the House of Commons 1792).
10. The intent is to distinguish those Socialists who are not a part of the international Communist conspiracy and those who dominate the various national socialist political parties of Western Europe, the Labour Party of Britain and the Congress Party of India.
11. The period comprehended runs from the stock market crash in 1929 until the beginnings of war preparations in 1938.
12. The reference is to the general theories with respect to the causes and cures of economic depressions as presented in Lord John M. Keynes's General Theory of Employment, Interest and Money and developed by the modern economists of the Keynesian school, such as J. K. Galbraith, P. A. Samuelson, and W. W. Rostow. Rexford Tugwell was probably the most significant in fastening this bias on the "New Deal."
13. Reference is to all those theories that seek a purely naturalistic concept of the society, the culture, and development. To achieve this, it becomes necessary to break down, reject, or otherwise deny all that sets man apart from other creatures.
14. Just as Marx had enshrined the economic drive as the controlling instinct, so Freud enshrined the sexual instinct. Characteristically, each proceed from his assumption and reasoned toward his preconceived conclusion.
15. "A successful resistance is a revolution, not a rebellion. Rebellion, indeed, appears on the back of a flying enemy, but revolution flames on the breastplate of the victorious warrior." John Wilkes's speech for American Colonies, House of Commons, February 6, 1775.
16. To the Christian, this begins with the death of Christ whereby man was restored to his freedom. To the Protestant, it involves the whole of the Reformation with the return to the scriptures for authority. For the Anglo-Saxon and the English-speaking nations, it is marked by the "Glorious Revolution" of

1688 that affirmed the subordination of the Crown to the parliament. All Americans can celebrate the glorious era of 1776 in the same tradition.
17. Successful examples are the "World Peace Council" set up in 1948, and the World Federation of Trade Unions. Further reference may be had to the list of subversive organizations published by the U.S. Attorney General.
18. The term "Liberal" is employed in its American and not European sense. What this means is that American Liberal does not subscribe to the traditional and classical European concept of removing restraints on individual liberty and the advancement of political democracy accompanied by an elimination of governmental control of commerce and industry. Liberal in the American tradition means the free use of governmental authority to control or to otherwise influence the activities of corporations that are not respected as performing a desirable purpose. Coincident with this anticorporate bias is a dedication to the advancement of certain collective groupings, such as what is termed *labor*, the *farmer, aged, youth, underprivileged, minority*, or any other vote heavy collective grouping to facilitate the increase in government and the expansion of power.
19. "Since the ultimate freedom of the person beyond all psychological, economic, political, geographic and other determining factors is always hidden and can be known only introspectively, and since every event or action once having taken place can be plausibly interpreted as the inevitable consequence of a previous event or action, there is a natural temptation for all students of historical events to be more deterministic than the facts warrant." Reinhold Niebuhr's essay on Freedom contained in *A Handbook of Christian Theology*, Fontana Books, 1960, p. 144.
20. For an example of the non-Conservative concept, we refer to Buckle, *History of Civilization in England* (N.Y., 1858), p. 14f. "Rejecting, then, the metaphysical dogma of free will . . . we are driven to the conclusion that the actions of men, being determined by their antecedents, must have a character of uniformity, that is to say, must, under precisely the same circumstances, always issue in precisely the same results." This line of reasoning leads to the non-Conservative conclusion that murder, rape, arson, etc., are all the product of the general social conditions the criminal performing the act under the compulsion of antecedents. Along with free will, individual responsibility is destroyed.
21. "The common man, finding himself in a world so excellent, technically and socially, believes that it has been produced by nature, and never thinks of the personal efforts of highly-endowed individuals which the creation of this world presupposed. Still less will he admit the notion that all these facilities

still require the support of certain difficult human virtues . . ." Jose Ortega y Gasset, *The Revolt of the Masses*, N.Y., 1932, p. 59–63. W.W. Norton & Co.
22. Much of the non-Conservative intellectual thought in recent years has had a tendency to view the modern corporation as a property-owning entity with interest that conflict with those of the "public." The intellectual seems oblivious of the corollary to the public institutionalized ownership.
23. "Practical ownership consists of a life interest, inalienable in most cases, and a reversion or remainder which again, when vested, is simply another life interest." Munroe Smith, *The Development of European Law*.
24. "The French nobility had stubbornly held aloof from the other classes and succeeded in getting themselves exempted from most of their duties to the community, fondly imagining they could keep their lofty status while evading obligations . . . The more their immunities increased, the poorer they became . . . they led nobody, they were alone, and when an attack was launched on them, their sole recourse was flight." Alexis de Tocqueville, *The Old Regime and the French Revolution*, trans. Stuart Gilbert, Doubleday Anchor Books, 1955.
25. "God, having made man such a creature that, in his own judgment, it was not good for him to be alone, put him under strong obligations of necessity, convenience, and inclination, to drive him into society . . ." John Locke, *Of Civil Government*, Ch. VII, Par. 77, "The End of Law."
26. "Property is the highest right a man can have to anything; being used for that right which one has to lands or tenements, goods, or chattels, which no way depends on another man's courtesy." Jackson ex dem. Paarson v. Housel, 17 Johns. 281, 283. This definition will suffice for the purposes of our discussion, but it should be recognized that in the earliest societies the concept of possession was distinguished from property. For that early treatment of this relationship in Common Law, see *The History of English Law, Second Edition*, Vol. II, Chapter IV, Ownership and Possession, pp. 1–183.
27. The term "rule of law" seems to have acquired a usage in recent years, which is substantially expanded beyond its original and traditional juristic meaning. Traditionally it has meant a "legal principle, of general application, sanctioned by the recognition of authorities, and usually expressed in the form of a maxim or logical proposition. Called a 'rule' because in doubtful or unforeseen cases it is a guide or norm for their decision." Touillier tit. Prel, no. 17, source *Black's Law Dictionary, Third Edition*. This concept has been borrowed and expanded upon by social philosophers to describe a system of authority in political order characterized by law as the guide as distinguished from the judgment of men. Frequently the term is employed to

described what the non-Conservative calls "Democracy" as a rule of law and not of men. This distinction seems to break down in these days of Judicial positivism where the United States Supreme Court can rely on the authority of G. Myrdal, a European political-economist to decide in May 1954 that the separate but equal doctrine under which segregated schools had operated for just short of a century was not contrary to the Fourteenth Amendment. When this is conserved alongside of the tendency to employ "legislative history" in construing the law as it is written, we seem to be heading full circle and when we are urged to "obey the supreme law of the land" we are in fact being urged to obey the rule of men and not law. It is for this reason that the term should be approached with extreme caution, and this is particularly so when it is extended in the international arena.

28. "The right of one or more persons to possession and use of a thing to the exclusion of others." Civil Code of the State of California, Sec. 654.

29. The term *unfree* is employed to distinguish between those peoples who find their freedoms restricted in the sense that they are denied liberty in one way or another through colonial rule, or an authoritarian rule, and those under Communist domination where freedom means "the recognition of necessity." Where necessity is determined by the party, the person is free whose entire personality is in harmony with the "necessity" so determined. Thus, the term *freedom* lacks an acceptable basis of positive and negative application in the Western sense and becomes a positive condition of individual denial in a state of being "unfree" in the Communist sense.

30. "All the ancient, honest, juridical principles and institutions . . . are so many clogs to check and retard the headlong course of violence and oppression. They were invented for this one good purpose, that what was not just should not be convenient." Edmund Burke, "Letter to John Farr and John Harris, Esq. (Sheriffs of the City of Bristol) on the Affairs of America," 1777.

31. Julius Horwitz, New York City Welfare investigator, and author of the novel *The Inhabitants*, on or about May 16, 1962, made the following remarks to the U.S. Senate Finance Committee with respect to public welfare. "The bit problem is the children born into a dismal wasteland whose landscape is defined by mental institutions, reformatories, adult prisons, the street . . . The birth of a child was beginning to emerge as the means for guaranteeing financial security and recognition to a growing group of young girls who themselves had grown up in dependency . . . their minds torn apart by the frightening environment that surrounds their welfare homes, have almost disrupted the New York school system." Testifying before the same committee, State Senator Henry A. Wise, Chairman of New York committee on public

welfare declared that "the dogmatic nonsense that has become social welfare doctrine is making slaves of thousands of people today—slaves in the prison of pauperism."

32. The first state laws limiting the hours of work for women and children in industry were passed in 1903 and rapidly were enacted in all jurisdictions.
33. "The first society was between man and wife, which gave beginning to that between parents and children . . ." John Locke, *Of Civil Government*, Book II, Ch. VII, par. 77.
34. Equality. "The condition of possessing substantially the same rights, privileges, and immunities, and being liable to substantially the same duties." *Louisville and N.R. Co. vs. Commonwealth*, 160 Ky 769, 170 S.W. 162.
35. Equity in its moral sense, "to live honestly, to harm nobody, to render to every man his due." Justinian Inst. 1,1,3.
    Equity in its jural sense, "(2) administers and adjusts common-law rights where the courts of common law have no machinery; (3) supplies a specific and preventative remedy for common law wrongs where courts of common law only give subsequent damages." Chute Eq. 4.
36. In recent years, the Federal Reserve System has become increasingly subject to the influences of the Executive with respect to discount rates, reserve ratios, and open-market policies. This tendency was substantially accelerated by the Employment Act of 1946.
37. Alexis de Tocqueville and Lord Acton early recognized the inherent contradiction in the philosophical framework of the French Revolution. Each understood the essential incompatibility of *égalité* and *liberté*. In modern discourse, this involves an understanding that social security and freedom are exclusive of each other.
38. "Knowledge and learning generally diffused through the community being essential to the preservation of a free government . . ." The Constitution of the State of Indiana (1816).
39. Speech on a Resolution to put Virginia into a State of Defense, Richmond, Virginia, March 23, 1775, Patrick Henry. "Is life so dear, or peace so sweet, as to be purchased at the price of chains and slavery? Forbid it, almighty God! I know now what course others may take but as for me, give me liberty or give me death."
40. This concept of inalienable rights and equality comprehended by the Declaration of Independence, composed under the guiding hand of Jefferson has been adopted by the non-Conservative Liberal as forever putting the stamp of social and rational optimism on the American system. The fact that the framers of the Constitution enumerated specific rights within the context

of that document and the first ten Amendments is an embarrassing paradox. It seems unnecessary to debate whether the praetorian aesthetic gentleman from Virginia was the "father of the liberty-democratic" tradition in America. The Declaration of Independence was a propaganda document designed to justify what must have been an agonizing decision among the colonists. The fact is that the idea of inalienable rights which corresponds to the nature of man and his natural condition is a useful idea to the Conservative. This embraces the idea that there exists a body of rights that no legitimate act of government may abridge. The Conservative can also accept the idea of equality so long as it is reconciled with the nonegalitarian concepts that underlie all Constitutional provisions.

41. The use of the term *justice* here employs the personification of the symbol of the blindfolded lady holding the scales high in her left hand and the sword in her right. The concept has to do with the ideas developed by Socrates in the Republic of Plato and of Aristotle as set out in his Nichomecean Ethics V, as incorporated within the Justinian's Institute book 1, title 1, grounded in the Christian ethic, and developed in its specific applications through the Anglo-American system of common law.
42. The concept is one of rendering unto every man his due, his regard or punishment according to the merits and without regard to his station or condition.
43. The term "equality" here comprehends equal protection in the sense of undiscriminating application, equal access to the mechanism through which justice is obtained and some reasonable degree of balance as between the parties.
44. This particular subject is given broad treatment in Equal Justice for the Accused by a Special Committee of The Association of the Bar of the City of New York and the National Legal Aid and Defender Association, Garden City, N.J. Doubleday and Co., 1959.
45. November 29, 1961, Associate Justice Tom C. Clark of the U.S. Supreme Court, addressing the Southwest Regional Seminar of State Trial Judges in Austin, Texas, announced a three-year, $348,000 grant from the W. K. Kellogg Foundation of Battle Creek, Michigan, to the Joint Committee for the effective administration of justice.
46. Attention is invited to the article "The Crisis in the Courts," *Fortune Magazine*, December 1961.
47. "Men living in democratic ages to not readily comprehend the utility of forms. Forms excite their contempt and often their hatred; as they commonly aspire to none but easy present gratifications, they rush onwards to the object

of their desires, and the lightest delay exasperates them. Forms become more necessary in proportion as the government becomes more active and more powerful, while private persons are becoming more indolent and more feeble. Thus the democratic nations naturally stand in more need of forms than other nations, and they naturally respect them less . . ." Alexis de Tocqueville, *Democracy in America*, New York, Vintage 1954 Book II, p. 343–348. Alfred A. Knopf, Inc.

48. Professor J.K. Galbraith, author of the bestseller *The Affluent Society*, advances the thesis that farmers' incomes have been raised through the farm subsidy program and, at the same time, asserts that there has not been any economic distortion through the diversion or mal-allocation of resources. This theory is based on the premise that the resources employed would not otherwise have been employed or would not otherwise have existed. Ref. "Economic Preconceptions and Farm Policy," American Economic Review, March 1953, p. 40f.

49. The reader's attention is drawn to the fact that then-President Eisenhower presented a budget with a slight surplus for the fiscal year July 1, 1961, to June 30, 1962, despite the fact that the country was in an economic recessionary period. The Eisenhower budget was based upon the belief that the economy left substantially to itself would right itself shortly. President Eisenhower proved correct. Most economists now calculate that the recession bottomed out in February 1962. President Kennedy took office one month earlier and armed with spend-for-prosperity schemes, unbalanced the budget to the tune of $6 billion, more or less. The Kennedy political economists will not be able to reasonably claim that the deficit actually stimulated business, but as of January 1962, we had already heard the claim of the psychological effect in anticipation.

50. "So far as the Sophists were concerned, they had no philosophy; they taught what well-to-do students were willing to pay for . . . Some of them at least stood for a new point of view . . . simply humanism—the twisting of knowledge toward man as its center." George H. Sabine, *A History of Political Theory*, May 1946, Henry Holt and Co., p. 27.

51. For further information on this particular subject, the reader's attention is directed to the publications of the American Institute for Economic Research, under the direction of E.C. Harwood, Great Barrington, Mass., and the National Bureau of Economic Research, N.Y.

52. The terms *maturity* and *take off* are those employed by W.W. Rostow, Professor of Economic History, MIT, in his book, *The Stages of Economic Growth*, Cambridge University Press, 1960. "Affluence" is to be understood in the

context used by Professor J.K. Galbraith, and "sustained economic growth" is my understanding of President Kennedy's meaning. That state where a community has achieved a capacity to generate its own capital formation for investment in additional production tools.

53. The bizarre, contorted technique of expression employed by the ruling elite in George Orwell's 1984, where peace becomes war, love is hate, etc. The characteristic is an indifference to the truth and a doctrinarian nationalization of everything, resolving all contradictions in favor of the dogma in an exercise where to will is to believe.

54. "Conservative Abundance" is defined as that condition of wealth at the command of a people to sustain their liberty. It is wealth that is the product of their industry and corresponds to their aspirations. It is the economic condition of dynamic equipoise characterized by a constantly shifting equilibrium between the requirements of individual people and the scarce resources available. It flows out of an atmosphere of individual competition constantly being resolved in conservative cooperation.

55. The Welfare State as it is understood by the author is related to the ideas of mixed economy, progressive capitalism, or state capitalism, with the emphasis upon government intervention and participation and a de-emphasis or moving away from private ownership of property. It is characterized by a political centralization of authority, and emphasis on Executive action. The interest and rights of the individual are progressively subordinated to the "general welfare" as articulated by the ruling elite and pursued in the name of "The People."

56. "It could be that the Federal Republic is now undermined beyond hope of restoration. It could also be that the American people have had more than they want of totalitarian democracy and are turning against it as they earlier turned against Jacobism." *Freedom and Federalism*, Felix Morley, Chicago, Henry Rignery Co., 1959.

57. J. M. Keynes, *General Theory of Employment, Interest, and Money*, Macmillan, London, 1936.

58. The term *full employment* is extremely vague in its connotation. It is employed by politicians and economists and labor union managers with little apparent consistency except to support the particular thesis they are advancing for the moment. For the purposes here intended, we shall rely on the concept implicit in the Employment Act of 1946.

59. "Easy money" refers to a general economic-credit condition created by the actions of the federal government through the implementation of fiscal policy maintaining interest rates below those that would prevail in the

unmanipulated money market and accompanied by federal guarantees of loans that work to make credit available to those whose risk potential would otherwise deny.
60. The term *labor union managers* is employed throughout these discussions to identify the ruling oligarchy of the American Trade Unions who have succeeded in perpetuating themselves in power from the rise of the unions to positions of power maturity. The similarity to the ruling oligarchies of American business corporations seems clear and thus the term *management* is deemed appropriate in either context.
61. *Free market* does not mean the unregulated laissez-faire market of the eighteenth century Liberal but implies sufficient regulation to maintain an atmosphere of constructive competition accompanied by an influence toward the diffusion of power so that concentrations do not develop such as to inhibit the individual exercise of his political, intellectual, economic, and religious liberties.
62. This general problem of facilitation breakup of the single faction oligarchic rule that characterizes the several collective institutions in our society should prove an area of fruitful Conservative study. I have reference to the business corporation, the farm cooperative, and the labor union.
63. *Realities*, No. 189, October 1961. "De L'automatisme a l'automation," p. 125.
64. For a clearer and penetrating consideration of the concept of obsolescence, the reader is directed to "The American Achievement" by Harold M. Fleming, published by the American Can Company, 1961.
65. Various retraining programs were underway as of the beginning of 1962 in the communities of Rhode Island through the State Department of Employment Security, in Huntington, West Virginia, Ansonia, Connecticut, and Pittsburgh, Pennsylvania.
66. This function has particular applicability to the central banking role and the requirement that the government servants do nothing that would cause and take all steps in their power to avoid a debasement of the exchange medium.
67. Dean Acheson, Secretary of State in 1950, overruled the position of the Joint Chief of Staff with respect to strong military aid to the Chinese Nationalist government and then stated that both Formosa and South Korea lay outside the United States' Pacific defense perimeter. Within six months, the Communists struck in South Korea.
68. Farewell address, President George Washington, September 17, 1796.

69. One example of this propensity for flight from reality into the dream world of fantasy is reflected by the position the Kennedy administration took with respect to the United Nations military action against the "secessionist" forces of Katanga in the Congo. The spokesman was the then-acting secretary of state, Mr. George Ball. Quoting the secretary of state, Mr. Rusk, Mr. Ball said on December 13, 1961, "Our (the United States) aim is the consolidation of the country (the area former known as the Belgian Congo) under a stable government which will pursue freely the true national interest of the Congolese. If Katanga is not peacefully integrated the Congo will face civil war and anarchy, and will be open to Communist penetration." With respect to the suggestion for a cease-fire between the battling forces of the UN and Katanga, Mr. Ball went on to say, "The attitude of the United States is simply this. We (the United States) want a cease-fire as soon as feasible. But we do not believe any cease-fire is feasible until the minimum objectives of the UN have been attained. There cannot be a repetition of the events of September when the United Nations was widely regarded as having suffered a defeat at the hands of the Katanga authorities and the situation further deteriorated." On December 14, 1961, *The New York Times* reported the concept of the United States interest in the UN military action against the Katanganese forces as expressed by a highly placed official as follows: "The fear that if the UN failed to achieve its purpose in the Congo, the world organization would never again be able to engage in a peace-keeping operation of this kind because member nations would refuse to make the necessary troops available. Thus," this official said, "the existence of the UN as an effective organization might well be at stake." It was in this atmosphere that Mr. Ball concluded his remarks explaining why the Kennedy administration opposed a cease-fire, with the words, "We hope and believe these objectives will be attained quickly and with a minimum loss of life and damage to property." (Note: AP dispatch of Dec. 13, 1961, from Elisabethville reported four Swedish SAAB Jet fighter-bombers attacked the center of the battered city with rockets and bombs. The UN with the transport facilities of fifteen Globemasters and two Hercules aircraft of the United States Air Force had deployed 4,500 troops to face a Katanga force of about 2,000. Mortar fire by the UN was reported as having killed 16 civilians and wounded 109. Katanganese Army casualties were reported as 14 dead and 78 wounded to date.)

Mr. Arthur Krock, columnist, *The New York Times*, dateline Washington, Dec. 13, 1961, noted the following points in relation to the Kennedy administration's "Congo policy." "Neither the United States nor the UN has published a blueprint of the 'loose confederation' of the Congo provinces that, if Tshombe rejected, would prove the unproved charge that he opposes any form of integration"; that the provincial subdivisions of the Congo are a colonial fiction, but are "absolutes in the integration concept of the UN and the United States"; that Tshombe had attended a UN sponsored "peace conference" outside the Congo where he "agreed with the other leaders to the loose confederation then proposed," but when he went to Coquilhatville, Congo, for ratification, "he was put under arrest by the central Government and not released until he had agreed to a dominant centralized regime. It is from this agreement under duress that Tshombe recanted." That the UN allegation that the present military operations were commenced upon discovery of "a secret military plan" of attack against the UN has been exposed and the plan was, in fact, a "defense plan instead against an expected UN attack on that province."

The Conservative conscience inquires, how many more lives are to be sacrificed to sustain the non-Conservative illusion that the UN is, or ever has been, a world organization capable of a "peace-keeping operation"? The United States government may very well be able to justify continued association with the United Nations Organization on the basis that such serves to advance the basic security interests of the United States, but this does not permit the support of the UN with the blood or the treasures of the American people, where support permits the UN to employ techniques and methods that are inconsistent with fundamental American principles and interests. A useful rule of thumb might be that we cannot support the UN in a collective action that we could not undertake on our own.

To clearly see the non-Conservative capacity for self-delusion, consider the casual manner in which the Kennedy administration withdrew promised air support from the ill-fated invasion of Castro's Cuba and assigned the survivors of the landing to the generous support given by the same administration to the use of Swedish and Indian jets to attack civilians in Elisabethville, meanwhile expressing the pious hope that there will result a "minimum loss of life."

The next question must be asked: what compelling security interest of the American people is involved that justified the decision to take but one life in its defense? Tell us, Mr. Kennedy, Mr. Rusk, Mr. Stevenson, and Mr. Ball, what was your justification for your decision to place the blood of Kataganese civilians on our hands?

We will not be diverted by pronouncements that if the UN was not allowed to avenge its defeat of September 1961, that it may "never again be able to engage in a peacekeeping operation of this kind." If the UN rests on such a foundation, that acceptance of a transient failure and the acknowledgement of error will topple it from its height, then we must say, let it fall of its own weight and disintegrate into rubble to be quickly swept into the ash can of history, lest its decaying structure engulf the world in a frantic effort to repair and salvage the debris.

Neither, Mr. President, will you cleanse our hands through a reference to a belated petition for a cessation of the attacks by the UN to "forestall actions that would tend to inflame passions as to jeopardize the chances of peace and reconciliation." The means will not be justified by the end.

70. This is somewhat difficult to square with the severe treatment accorded to Trujillio's regime in the Dominican Republic, but this, the "double standard," is characteristic of non-Conservative values. It would be almost ludicrous were it not so tragic to hear one group of non-Conservatives accusing others of the employment of the "double standard" of judgment, such as that following the "nonaligned" conference in Belgrade in 1961 and the Indian military seizure of the Portuguese enclaves in December of that year.

71. "Turn the people and the money loose and they will make the country strong." Dr. Ludwig Erhard, Economics Minister, German Federal Republic, speaking to the German people in a radio address announcing the end of rationing in 1948. Source: *New York Times*, International Edition, January 9, 1962.

72. "They have driven man from the civilization of the Twentieth Century into a condition of barbarism worse than the Stone Age ... what a monstrous absurdity and perversion of the truth it is, to represent the Communist theory as a form of progress, when, at every step and at every stage, it is simply marching back into the Dark Ages." Winston Churchill at Sunderland, January 3, 1921.

73. "We have before us an ordeal of the most grievous kind ... you ask, what is our aim? I can answer in one word: It is victory, however long and hard the road may be; for without victory there is no survival." Winston Churchill, addressing the House of Commons on May 13, 1940. Source: British Parliamentary Debates, House of Commons (Mansard, London, 1903–1940).

74. "The Party has stronger foundations than the State organs. It arose and exists not as a result of obligations of a legal order. Its development was called for by circumstances derived from political concepts, and mankind will always be in need of moral factors." Khrushchev reaffirmed this doctrine in 1958 first put forth by V. I. Lenin. (Ref. *Selected Works* N.Y. International Publishers, 1937. Vol. VI, p. 17).

75. The reader is invited to draw his own conclusions from the agreements concluded by the Roosevelt Administration at Yalta and Cairo, the Truman Administration at Potsdam, the Kennedy Administration's acquiescence to the isolation of East Berlin through the construction of the wall, and the picture of Khrushchev at Camp David and touring the United States as the guest of the Federal Government during the Eisenhower Administration.

76. "In a Democracy, the real rulers are the dexterous manipulators of votes, with their placemen, the mechanics who so skillfully operate the hidden springs which move the puppets in the arena of democratic elections. Men of this kind are ever ready with loud speeches lauding equality; in reality, they rule the people as any despot or military dictator might rule it." Konstantin Petrovich Pobiedonostev, *Moscow Conversations*. Translated as *Reflections of a Russian Statesmen*, R.C. Long, London, 1898.

INDEX

A

abstract terminology, use in politics of, 15, 17
Acheson, Dean, 146, 206
Adams, John
  Defense of the Constitution, 30
Adams, John Quincy
  Letters of Publicola, 30
Affluent Society, The (Galbraith), 88, 104, 115, 204
American Revolution, 28-29
automation, 128-29, 131

B

balance of payments, 156, 158, 160-61
Ball, George, 207
Bell, David E., 117
Bismarck, Otto von, 135
Burke, Edmund, 25, 29, 190
Burton, Richard F., 197

C

Churchill, Winston, 141, 190
Clark, Tom C., 203
Clausewitz, Carl von, 141
Clayton Act of 1914, *54*

Colonial Rebellion. *See* American Revolution
Common Market, 161-62
Common Sense (Paine), 30
Communism, 32, 40, 145-46, 165-68, 171-73, 175-79
Communist Front, 32
Communist Manifesto, The (Marx), 80
conservation, concept of, 32, 34
Conservative abundance, 60, 86, 90, 93-94, 97-98, 205
Conservative competition, 60, 187
Conservative society, 83, 125, 138, 140, 184
counterrevolution, 165-75, 177-78, 180-82
countervailing force, 81, 120
Currie, Lauchlin, 117

D

Darwinian theories, 27, 198
Das Kapital (Marx), 80
Declaration of Independence, 74, 203
Defense of the Constitution (John Adams), 30
Diebold, John, 129
doublethink, 93, 105, 205

E

easy money, 89, 91, 101, 205
economic growth, 85, 94, 97
economics, as a discipline, 86-87
Eisenhower, Dwight David, 148, 204
Employment Act of 1946, 101, *202, 205*
equality, 7, 59, 69, 74-77, 81, 105, 126, 155-56, 202-3
equity, 51-53, 55-56, 65, 67, 202
European Economic Community (EEC), 99

F

family, 63, 202
Farewell Address (Washington), 30, 206
Federal Reserve System, 52, 89, 202
foreign aid, 93, 96, 151-52, 154, 156-57, 169
freedom, 18-19, 185, 201
free market, 91, 98, 102-3, 160-61
Freud, Sigmund, 198
Freudian bias, 27, 198
fringe benefits, 127-28, 134
full employment, 85, 88, 101-2, 113, 205

G

Galbraith, J. K., 88, 116, 198, 204-5
  The Affluent Society, 104, 115
Gaulle, Charles de, 179
General Agreement on Tariffs and Trade (GATT), 164
General Theory, 27, 100, 113, 116, 198
general will, 18, 120, 197
genius, definition of, 83
Goldberg, Arthur J., 108-9, 112
government, roles of, 77-82
Great Depression, 27, 87, 89, 135-36, 198

H

Hamilton, Fowler, 151
hardcore unemployed, 105
Harder, D. S., 129
Heller, W. W., 117
Henry, Patrick, 71
Hitler, Adolf, 179
Holmes, Oliver, Jr., 150
Horwitz, Julius
  The Inhabitants, 201
human nature, 20-22, 24

I

idealism, 33
inalienable rights, 7, 29-30, 47, 63, 74, 80, 141, 202-3
individual mobility, 123, 126-27
inflation, 89-93, 95, 101-2, 105, 111, 114, 116, 118, 138, 169
Inhabitants, The (Horwitz), 201

J

jabberwocky, 179
Jefferson, Thomas, 8, 72, 202
justice, 75, 77, 137, 141, 172, 203

K

Kennedy, John F., 108, 114, 148, 151, 204
Keynes, John M., 99-100, 117, 198
Keynesian theory. *See* General Theory
Krock, Arthur, 207

L

labor productivity, 108
Labor unions, 124
Letters of Publicola (John Quincy Adams), 30
Liberal, 199
liberty, 20, 24, 39-44, 47, 81, 139, 143-45, 185
Lincoln, Abraham, 78-79, 190
Lord Acton, 50, 202

M

Madison Papers, 30
Marshall Plan, 154
Marx, Karl, 198
   The Communist Manifesto, 80
   Das Kapital, 80
Marxian Socialism, 27
Mr. Spivak, 151
myth-think, 147, 179

N

necessity, 198
neutralism, 171, 175

P

Paine, Thomas, 92
   Common Sense, 30
Peron, Juan, 115
Phalanx, 179
Plato, 23, 203
private ownership of property
   corporate form of, 53, 55
   definition of, 201
   and individual liberty, 134
   as part of Conservative structure, 38-39
   and right to the benefits from the ownership, 48-49
   using police power
      to ensure health, 42-43
      to ensure public welfare, 43, 45
      to ensure safety, 41
property, 60, 200
pump-up theory, 116

R

Red Army, 9, 148, 178
Reuther, Walter, 109, 124
Roosevelt, Franklin D., 87, 144-46, 190
Rostow, W. W., 198, 204
Rule of Law, 24-25, 29, 39, 163, 172, 200

S

safety, definition of, 41
Samuelson, P. A., 116, 198
Schlesinger, Arthur, Jr., 116-17
security
   definition of, 139
   of the state, 141
selection system, 51
self-discipline, 24
self-help, 133
Sherman Antitrust Act of 1890, *53*
Smith, Adam, 116
   The Wealth of Nations, 117
social order, birth of, 39
Social Security Act, 134-37, 139
society, 26
Sorenson, Theodore C., 117

spend for prosperity, 87, 89, 100-101
stereotypes, 15

T

Tocqueville, Alexis de, 202
trickle-down theory, 115
Truman, Harry, 144-46, 159
Tugwell, Rexford, 198

U

underemployment, 87-88, 100-102, 104-7, 121-23
unemployment, 87, 100, 102, 104, 113, 115, 121, 127-28, 131-34
United Nations (UN), 12, 93, 143-50, 175
United States Constitution, 25-26, 141, 197

W

Washington, George, 147
    Farewell Address, 30
Wealth of Nations, The (Smith), 117
Wedemeyer, Albert C., 145
welfare state, 80, 94, 99, 108, 169, 205
White, Harry Dexter, 117
Wilson, Charles E., 123-24
Wilson, Thomas W., 144, 180
Wise, Henry A., 202
wish-think, 101, 179
world opinion, 172-73